LOOKING FOR TIFFANY
A JOURNEY INTO THE PRESENCE OF GOD

Tiffany = Presence or Manifestation of God, Appearance of God, Mark of God, Revelation of God.

- A training regimen for the spiritual triathlon ahead to gain discernment of God's voice and presence.

- A story bringing you from seed to blossoming rose; you will find yourself going from a black-and-white two-dimensional space into blooming in full color as you plant, uproot, and flourish in your daily life while reading and working your way through this book.

- A journey of growth, an immersion into the ocean to be refreshed and cleansed by the water, then climb aboard a small canoe to float down the river, learning to flow with the Holy Spirit, then step out on dry ground and walk the winding Narrow Path into the garden where you begin to blossom, flourishing into the fruitful garden you were created to become.

*Show me the right path, O Lord; point out the road for me to follow. Lead me by your truth and teach me, for you are the God who saves me. - **Psalm 25:4 NLT***

Tears of joy will stream down their faces, and I will lead them home with great care. They will walk beside quiet streams and on smooth paths where they will not stumble. For I am Israel's father, and Ephraim is my oldest child.

*- **Jeremiah 31:9 NLT***

Trust in the Lord with all your heart; do not depend on your own understanding. Seek his will in all you do, and he will show you which path to take.

*- **Proverbs 3:5-6 NLT***

*He renews my strength. He guides me along right paths, bringing honor to his name. - **Psalm 23:3 NLT***

*You make known to me the path of life; you will fill me with joy in your presence, with eternal pleasures at your right hand. - **Psalm 16:11 NIV***

The Lord directs the steps of the godly. He delights in every detail of their lives. Though they stumble, they will never fall, for the Lord holds them by the hand.

*- **Psalm 37:23-24 NLT***

This is what the Lord says:

*"Stop at the crossroads and look around. Ask for the old godly way, and walk in it. Travel its path, and you will find rest for your souls" ....- **Jeremiah 6:16 NLT***

I will teach you wisdoms ways and lead you in straight paths.

*- **Proverbs 4:11 NLT***

*Look straight ahead, and fix your eyes on what lies before you. Mark out a straight path for your feet; stay on the safe path. Don't get sidetracked; keep your feet from following evil. - **Proverbs 4:25-27 NLT***

I will lead blind Israel down a new path, guiding them along an unfamiliar way. I will brighten the darkness before them and smooth out the road ahead of them.

-Isaiah 42:16 NLT

The Lord is good and does what is right; he shows the proper path to those who go astray.

-Psalm 25:8 NLT

People from many nations will come and say, "Come, let us go up to the mountain of the Lord, to the house of Jacob's God. There he will teach us his ways, and we will walk in his paths." For the Lord's teaching will go out from Zion; his word will go out from Jerusalem.

-Isaiah 2:3 NLT

Who are those who fear the Lord? He will show them the path they should choose.

– Psalm 25:12 NLT

The Lord says,

Then I will heal you of your faithlessness; my love will know no bounds, for my anger will be gone forever. I will be to Israel like a refreshing dew from Heaven. Israel will blossom like the lily; it will send roots deep into the soil like the cedars in Lebanon. Its branches will spread out like beautiful olive trees, as fragrant as the cedars of Lebanon. My people will again live under my shade. They will flourish like grain and blossom like grapevines. They will be as fragrant as the wines of Lebanon. "O Israel, stay away from Idols! I am the one who answers your prayers and cares for you. I am like a tree that is always green; all your fruit comes from me." Let those who are wise understand these things. Let those with discernment listen carefully. The paths of the Lord are true and right. And righteous people live by walking in them. But in those paths, sinners stumble and fall.

-Hosea 14:4-9 NLT

CONTENTS

DEDICATION

This work is dedicated to:

The Great King of all the Earth Emmanuel

Yeshua Son of the Living God

"The harvest is great, but the workers are few. So pray to the Lord who is in charge of the harvest; ask him to send more workers into his fields."

-Luke 10:2 NLT

Many notable people have planted seeds, encouraged, and inspired me to go higher throughout my life, and although I cannot name them all, I choose to give the highest honor and recognition to many who invest their time, love, and money often without honor and recognition.

Many more unnamed friends that have encouraged, inspired, shared, and/or dedicated their lives to Jesus, and the Lord has chosen to honor me to work beside them. I call these special ones my Mark 3:33 Kingdom Family. To the ones I have served with past, present, and future, it's truly an honor, and I dedicate this book to you all.

"Jesus replied, 'Who is my mother? Who are my brothers?' Then he looked at those around him and said, 'Look, these are my mother and brothers. Anyone who does God's will is my brother and sister and mother.'"

- Mark 3:33-35 NLT

My Family, Jim, Hayden, and Natalie

My Bonus Children

My Mom Myra

My Dad Jim

My Siblings Laura and James "Randy"

My Beloved Joy Bassett

My Beloved Angie Thompson

My Wing Man Heather Squires

My Mentor, Aja McCombs

My Coach, Pastor Rick Mendoza

My Prayer Partners -The Abided Ones

Mr. Surf John and Libby Johnson

My Friend Susan Palacios

My Friends Robert and Paige James

My Friends Rochelle and Michael Tierney

My Friends The Grube Family

My Friends Alexa, Frannie and Kim

My Friends Tiger, Pam, Tia, Nelda, Diane, and Linda

My Friends Glenna, Shelly, Sue, and Lynda

All My Brittany, Britni, Britney(ies)

All My Mark Kingdom Family

So, we have not stopped praying for you since we first heard about you. We ask God to give you complete knowledge of his will, spiritual wisdom, and understanding. Then, how you live will always honor, and please the Lord and your lives will produce every kind of good fruit. All the while, you will grow as you learn to know God better and better. We also pray that you will be strengthened with all his glorious power and have all the endurance and patience you need. May you be filled with joy, and may you always thank the Father. He has enabled you to share in the inheritance that belongs to his people, who live in the light. He has rescued us from the Kingdom of darkness and transferred us into the Kingdom of his dear Son, who purchased our freedom and forgave our sins.

Colossians 1:9-14 NLT

FOREWORD

On a hot summer's day, as the community gathered for a monthly night of music, food, and fellowship, I worked side by side with my husband, shaking lemonade in a booth. Many people passed by, and I recognized Sara George's daughter. As the night was closing, my husband said he saw a woman he did not know and had never met pass by our lemonade stand. Something unique about her stood out. She was flowing through the crowd, and as I spotted her, I saw the glory of the Lord following her, with a group of students trailing behind her. I could see joy in their smiles and hear their laughter, and I understood they were here with a purpose from the Lord. I immediately knew and responded that it was Sara George.

Cody and Brittany Lee

PREFACE

Jesus spoke to the people once more and said, "I am the light of the world. If you follow me, you won't have to walk in darkness because you will have the light that leads to life." -John 8:12 NLT

GOLDEN HOUR

The sunset is a time of beauty and golden reflection, and it seems the sun is closer to us as it sinks into the horizon. The sunset effect is caused by light scattering into more of the atmosphere. The best light exists right before the sun goes down, and the day fades, so it will be when the hour of the Earth draws to a close. It's a time when, although it's almost dark, all eyes are on the son. Jesus will radiate perfect light and be reflected into the atmosphere. The reflection of colors in the sky will bring a subtle beauty to the landscape, as it will be with his beautiful brides. They will radiate color, creativity, and beauty into their communities. This light makes people glow golden and will be cast upon His chosen for a season before the night falls.

There is a moment in time predestined from the beginning where all of creation would be mesmerized by the Son. He will be the focal point. All eyes will look upon His colorful beauty and reflect Him while resting in Him, just as watching a sunset requires intentionally slowing down and making space to relax. Sitting in His presence will allow us to be more intentional in resting, enabling us to receive His peace and causing stress and anxiety to burn off. Before the sun sets and darkness takes over, this golden hour of time is called "Glory Hour." This beautiful glory hour was scheduled for a particular moment in history. As it gets darker on the Earth, remember that the end of the day must be approaching, but in that unique space and moment, the colors are captivating, and many will stop, pause, and look at the Son, resting and reflecting in his glory. They will see Him and His brilliance. This moment will be marked by people slowing down their schedules and itineraries; priorities will be shifted and traded for a much slower pace. Many will rush towards Jesus, and He will shine. The more the people look, the more they will become like him. They will be like the waters during sunset, reflecting His brilliance and bringing color across the Earth. When the night comes, His people will shine like stars. These flaming ones will spin, and as they move, His light upon them will increase, reflecting Jesus in the likeness of a diamond shimmering and reflecting light like stars twinkling in the night. In the twilight, the spinning will cause sparks to shoot off, like shooting stars releasing sparks and setting the globe on fire. At this moment, many signs, wonders, and miracles will mark Glory Hour.

Let's start preparation now. Why wait? The time is drawing near. Join me in the pages ahead, discover the well-lit narrow path where we align, and remove everything hiding His treasure within you— that bountiful treasure box inside you of the most beautiful golden glory.

Scripture References
Luke 4:40, Psalm 67, Revelation 2:28, Revelation 21:11, 23,
Revelation 22:3-5,16
Reference YouTube <u>The Sunset – Golden Glory Hour Sara George's Love</u>
<u>Notes from Heaven:</u>

<u>https://www.youtube.com/watch?v=FKvLC_etbFcc&t=22s</u>

INTRODUCTION

The meanings of the name Tiffany = Presence or manifestation of God, Appearance of God, Mark of God, Revelation of God.

This book title was birthed from a dream. In the dream, I was looking for Tiffany. In the dream, Tiffany was a friend and former neighbor. When I started trying to understand what the dream meant, I discovered the meaning of the name Tiffany. Tiffany represents the manifested presence of God. I was, and still am, in a season of spiritual growth taking me places; it's taking me on a journey of seeking and following the Holy Spirit. I want to dive deep. It's a season where we are called deeper.

It's God's privilege to conceal things and the king's privilege to discover them.

-Proverbs 25:2 NLT

As the deer longs for streams of water, so I long for you, O God.

-Psalm 42:1 NLT

I thirst for God, the living God. When can I go stand before Him?

- Psalm 42:2 NLT

Deeper calleth unto deep at the noise of thy waterspouts: all thy waves and thy billows are gone over me. -Psalm 42:7 KJV

Deep is calling to take you deeper. It's the looking to go deeper in my relationship with God at a greater level of being led by his spirit, the more of God, desiring to be anywhere God is present. Of course, he is everywhere, but sometimes, we can go into a place where the atmosphere has been cleansed through prayer and worship, and many people who have discernment can tangibly feel and experience his companionship in these places. In this book, it may be fun to refer to seeking his manifested presence as Tiffany. Let's look for Tiffany together.

In the Old Testament, the Israelites often set up a stone or an altar at a place of encounter with the Lord. Its purpose was to remind them of the things God did for them. They saw the altar and talked about what had transpired or told stories about their generational history, often as verbal traditions.

I can imagine that, as a tribe or family traveled by foot, donkey, or some other primitive means, they may have intentionally stopped at altars to rest. It would remind them to worship the living God. It reminded them to tell their children how good and mighty the Great I AM was to their people. They talked about their supernatural encounters so they would not forget Him. God wants to be remembered. I searched my life and thought about what a modern-day altar would look like. Would it be some rocks stacked somewhere, or a statue? Then I considered what types of altars I would build or how I could remember Jesus and pass this family legacy of stories down to my children to continue the tradition. I believe this book will serve as a written altar in my life, a place to remember and pass on a legacy of the presence of God. I dreamed of writing a book as a child and often responded "author" when asked what I wanted to be when I grew up. Then, it was as if the reality of making a living or raising a family hindered the pursuit.

As I journey into the presence of God, I am discovering that my blueprints from Heaven say "AUTHOR," so I am trying to discern what it looks like to "write a book." How do you start something new that you haven't ever accomplished before? The publishing process seemed intimidating, and English class wasn't my favorite subject. BUT GOD provides the wisdom and grace, so it's a challenge I am willing to accept. Everyone is called to a higher purpose and destiny. Perhaps it just takes Faith and trust in the Lord. He says the Faith of a mustard seed can move mountains. Maybe a grain of salt can write a book.

I'm writing this book out of obedience to my Heavenly Father. He wanted to write a book and asked me to partner with Him. It will be an asset to those seeking to understand how to teach others how to listen and follow the Holy Spirit into the Presence of God while encouraging them with some short faith-building stories and humor. Some of my childhood favorites, such as Anne of Green Gables and Little Women, inspire me to share my testimonies. This book is not intended to be my full testimony but simply some short stories to encourage. This book will answer some questions to gain understanding and teach others how to position themselves in the heavenly realm to receive revelation and instruction, which will become increasingly critical in the coming age.

The presence of God changes everything. Join me in igniting the voice of God in this generation. In Acts 4:13, the disciples were recognized as ordinary men filled with the Holy Spirit. The Holy Spirit inside them stirred up their communities. I pray this book stirs hearts to action in communities so that it will be said this generation looks like those who have been with Jesus. Let's shake the nations together in unified devotion to our Creator and Redeemer through the Blood of Jesus.

Once again I will shake not only the earth but the heavens also.

- Hebrews 12:26 NLT

It is time to become BOLD. He spits out the lukewarm. Do not be ashamed of the gospel. We are called to be the body with Christ as the head. We will be used as a lighthouse, with Christ as the light source within us. Christianity is more than teaching or listening. It is actively seeking a relationship and the presence of the Lord. I see this book as a bite of fruit from the living vine. Let it nourish you from the inside out. You have the choice to plant the seeds and grow a tree of Faith in your life, spit the seeds out if they do not apply to you, or keep two and throw one away. Let the Holy Spirit guide you through the pages and navigate your thoughts as you float down the stream on this journey.

CHAPTER 1

WELCOME TO THE OCEAN
THERE'S NO TIME TO LOSE. DIVE IN!

God searches our hearts for the pure ones desiring to advance His Kingdom and bring Heaven to Earth with love and compassion. When He finds a heart ready to mature and ripen, He starts to call our name, and as we hear Him call, we respond: Here I am; where are You? I hear You calling me... and He responds, it's time to go deeper.

Put on your new nature and be renewed as you learn to know your creator and become like him. - *Colossians 3:10 NLT*

Come over close, and let's build a fire, sit, and reflect in the warmth of the flames.

If you are cold, you are too far from the fire of God; the flesh tries to finish what God started, so let's get closer and hotter together.

God searches our hearts for the pure ones desiring to advance His Kingdom and bring Heaven to Earth with love and compassion. When He finds a heart ready to mature and ripen, He starts to call our name, and as we hear Him call, we respond: Here I am, where are you? I hear you calling me. He responds it's time to go deeper. Chase My voice, follow Me, and I will teach you what it means to abide. When these hearts join forces, they become a chosen called-out tribe, and they persevere, determined to keep their eyes on Him. His sons and daughters come into the light of His love, surrendering everything and trading it all to abide in Him. When we, as His army, arise as a pure-hearted group determined to live in His presence, obeying His every command, we will see the victory of Heaven come to life on earth.

I see an army. It is a glowing group of warriors with their swords drawn marching forward. When I look to see the faces, all I see is Jesus. Each person has chosen to surrender their life unto the Lord Jesus Christ, and God has done work inside them, removing all darkness and bringing them into the DNA of Heaven. Each one reflects Jesus. Jesus left this Earth and has been waiting for His army of willing vessels to take their place, allowing Him to walk through their lives and raise them into mature, transformed sons and daughters.

Visualize you and me as Jesus. When Jesus walked through a community, people gathered. As He walked, He released signs, wonders, and miracles. Can you imagine Jesus walking through your town for a moment? Now imagine Jesus MULTIPLIED. What would it look like if a great army of Jesuses walked this earth? Consider how

3

it might turn the world upside down. Imagine miracles being an everyday occurrence, bringing many to testify of encountering Jesus and how those testimonies would quickly amplify and increase the Kingdom of God, just like the story about the woman at the well going into her community and bringing people to meet Jesus. I believe that has been His plan all along. He left knowing He would be reflected and multiplied on the Earth. When we bow low and allow Christ to grow and develop within us, He pushes out darkness and heals pain, transforming us into a new creation, and the old man, "human nature," dies. Jesus takes over our body, and as we surrender and permit Him, we become the temple of the living God. Our spirit becomes one with Jesus, leading the way instead of our carnal nature. It won't be you praying and ministering; instead, it's Jesus in you breathing, moving, and serving. We become Jesus to the masses. Visualizing ourselves as Jesus, Jesus living inside us, we are simply the clay shell, and when we surrender our life to Him and die to ourselves, He is taking our place. This should encourage you. It increases your Faith in knowing it isn't you—no more pressure. You are simply an eyewitness watching Jesus shine through you.

*Don't copy the behavior and customs of this world, but let God transform you into a new person by changing the way you think. Then you will learn to know God's will for you, which is good and pleasing and perfect. – **Romans 12:2 NLT***

Believe and recognize the power in the name of Jesus Christ of Nazareth (Yeshua)! The Holy Spirit has access to spiritual and legal rights to enter and influence our lives when we accept Jesus. The Holy Spirit will write the Laws of God in our hearts and minds. He will patiently and persistently pursue you until you desire to go to the next level of glory by making Him your Lord, Master, and King. Let me explain a vision I was given to understand what happens when we accept salvation. It's as if we ate a piece of fruit from the vine in John chapter 15.

I see the fruit on the branches, and as we accept the gift of salvation, we swallow the seeds in the fruit. The seeds can remain dormant for an extended period until the Father breathes onto the seeds and fills you with His Holy Spirit. He compels you to seek and ask to receive the baptism of the Holy Spirit. Fire baptism can be accepted only through the Holy Spirit. One example in the Bible is having a Holy Spirit-filled believer lay hands on another, asking God to use them as conduits to impart His Holy Spirit and fill them. God knows the desire and motives of your heart. If you have not yet experienced a Holy Spirit baptism, pray and ask the Father to direct your path to receive this Holy Spirit baptism.

You will recognize another believer by the fruit of their spirit. When someone accepts Christ, there will be transformation. Conversion to Christ Jesus results in a gradual heart transformation. It is much more than a decision of logic. Salvation is giving the deed to our heart to Jesus. He wants to reconcile us to Himself to plant a garden within us. Our hearts represent a piece of earth ready to be prepared for a garden, so the gardener needs to make changes. He has to work the ground, removing the top growth of grass, weeds, rocks, and debris. He needs to dig deeper into the soil until He has excellent, clean, soft, fertile ground to sow His seed.

Many people profess to believe without surrendering or yielding to the transformation. They claim they have given the deed of their hearts to Jesus, but looking at the ground, it still looks like a wild field untilled and hard. There is a point on the journey that you realize it's about putting your plans on an altar, realizing Jesus had no goals to advance Himself when He came to Earth. Instead, He gave His life to provide us with the Kingdom of God. It's a place of recognizing Jesus is Lord of ALL, and it's worth the price. It is an honor to sacrifice our self to become humble servants and see one more life enter those heavenly gates. There is a call to pick up the cross and continue advancing the Kingdom in the place where others died a martyr's death. Are we willing to carry out the mission as a living sacrifice?

When identifying the ones who have made a conversion versus a decision, look for the fruit. Fruit will not exist because a believer thinks they can buy salvation or a ticket to Heaven through striving to do good works, but instead, because God is good and the Holy Spirit's instructions, assignments, and teaching cannot produce bad fruit. He desires to continually teach and prune us through discipline to produce more fruit. The fruit of a mature believer will always be rooted in love. In some seasons of our lives, we may try to complete the work of the Holy Spirit in our flesh, which causes our motives and intentions to be out of alignment with Heaven. Ask the Holy Spirit if your roots are seeded from love. Anything dead or dying must be cut off to make room for new growth. There is no condemnation if you discover something isn't aligned with love, but God desires to correct those motives gently. Sometimes, we must have weeds pulled out of our hearts to allow God to plant new seeds of love. Remove the fruit that doesn't satisfy to create an infrastructure to support the upcoming abundant harvest.

God's ways are higher than ours, and as we mature in Christ, we understand that even the most intelligent human is still simply a mustard seed in comparison to the vast wisdom of our Creator. We cannot rely solely on our own experience, just like we can't rely on our emotions. We shouldn't assume that our experience is the only way God moves. This can cause disunity and separation among friends and Christ's followers. We must refrain from making judgments from our own experiences and instead realize God has given us a way to see Him in other people. God's way is to look at the fruit in the person or ministry and recognize that there will be differences, but we can pray and trust God to reveal Himself instead of separating ourselves and casting judgement. Choose to unify the body of Christ through love.

Let me give you an analogy to explain the different types or levels of relationships people have as Christians. Visualize God as a person on earth. You may not see Him, but He is omnipresent and able to be with you here in this earthly realm, so now I want you to picture Him as if He is living in your home. There are many different types of relationships between friends and family, and God the Father sets the supreme example of a PERFECT Father. He can be someone you know intimately, like your spouse or best friend, or He can be like an acquaintance you know from school or work, or He can live in the same house and never have a meaningful conversation with you. If He's an acquaintance, you know His name and might think He's a pretty cool guy, but He isn't someone you call after school to hang out with like you would a friend in your inner circle. If He's your best friend, you can't wait for free time to just tell Him about your day or sit and hang out with Him. Best friends are always there and make you feel like there is nowhere they would rather be than with you. The best friend is always interested in what God is doing. The best friend searches for Him when He doesn't answer his call. The best friend wants to attend all performances, sporting events, premieres, or whatever He does. The best friend goes to watch or participate as often as possible. Then, some relationships are lukewarm and are in the middle of best friends or acquaintans.

Here's another example. Consider that there are parents who helicopter around their children. They are involved and know all of their kids' friends by name and are intentional in scheduling time for vacations, dinners, and special events, and then some parents are distant. Maybe they work a lot of hours and find it awkward to connect with their kids, but in both analogies, if you ask the parents if they love their kids, they will say yes. There are also families where parents are the solid authoritarian type who require their kids to respect and fear them. That reminds me of religion. The religious mindset wants respect and fear without the relationship, and the involved parent believes you honor, fear, and respect someone you are in a loving relationship with. By showing honor to each other, we allow each other to grow in character, becoming honorable. (Honor is required for growth. Dishonor builds up pride making one unable to be taught by those they do not honor. Pride turns into stubbornness and rebellion closing one's heart and mind.) Think about a helicopter mom who let go of her son so he can turn into a man. It's natural to have a boy pull away from his mother. The mother, who has a close relationship with her kids, understands the natural transition, but while he grows, she watches and waits for the son to invite her back into his life. She may spend years waiting for that phone call, dinner, or coffee invitation, and she can't contain her excitement when it comes. She wants it to continue but knows she can't force or push her son into more time. Nevertheless, she waits because of her intense love for her child. She would spend as much of her time with him as HE allowed.

Then there is the "Karen" mom who forces her way into the child's life and, in turn, often causes rebellion to rise in the same way as a disciplinarian. Kids push away instead of drawing closer. Sometimes, returning to an intimate relationship with parents takes years, with some children transitioning into maturity sooner than others. Like earthly parents, God our Father and the Father of Yeshua is also waiting and watching. He created us to choose Him and will not force us to want to be near Him. He sees the ones who are immature and make mistakes but understands that many learn by the hands-on approach to life and he's always there waiting. He's waiting. I believe that today, just like the age at which children move out of their parent's home, it has increased to 30 something instead of eighteen. God is watching His kids, who appear physically able and old enough, still behaving like a child who never took steps to develop by moving out on their own. This is like the ones who have gone to church on Sunday for 30 years but still see Him as an acquaintance. They claim to love Him and possibly attend church and know His name, but they have never read the Bible for themselves. They rely on pastors and teachers to have a relationship with Him without desiring one themselves. I propose that it isn't enough to see a cool kid in class and hear all about what He's like, but if you don't call Him up and hang out with Him, He's not your friend. You might like Him and think He's cool, but when you get to Heaven one day, He will say He never knew you. It's time to make the King of Kings your "Best Friend." Like a mother who has given her son room to grow, He is waiting for you to seek Him. Seek Him, and He will come to you like a mother waiting to reunite with her son. The good news is it's never too late to call His number and invite Him over. I hope these words inspire you to desire a hunger and thirst for the Kingdom of Heaven. Be encouraged. Those who hunger and thirst for Him will be satisfied and see Him face to face. Psalm 17:14-15, Revelations 22:4, 17.

For the ones who receive revelation visually, I had a vision given to me to explain this concept differently. It is simply a visual aid or an image I received explaining the Christian growth cycle and should not be confused with doctrine or theology. Mothers may relate to this example. Visualize each person who receives salvation as the mother of Jesus. (I do not believe we are all Mary; this is simply a visual tool or exercise to gain a new perspective.) Each person receiving the seed of God carries Jesus until they allow Him to be birthed into their body. Jesus started the size of a tiny seed, then a bean, all the while feeling and hearing His heartbeat and movement deep within our womb. The difference in this spiritual Baby Jesus is there is no set time for the birth. He grows only as He is fed, and He starts to transform as the breath of God blows. He isn't forceful but instead waits for permission. He only grows to the point where we make room for Him. As we surrender each area of our hearts and lives, He gains mobility, and we start to feel Him in more substantial ways. I see instead of birthing a newborn, Jesus waits to step out until He is fully grown. Imagine the only way for Him to come oozing out of our very being, which is for Him to be the only thing inside. I see a man of light inside our earthly flesh growing and glowing as He shifts and moves things in His way. His body is growing and pushing out every dark moment in our lives. He pushes every hurt, pain, trauma, and sin out as He grows. He grows only to the point we give permission, but He desires to remove it all. He desires to grow until His foot of brilliant light fills our feet and His hands extend into our hands, His head pushing up in height until His eyes match our eyes, His ears become our ears, and then we give Him our voice, and He speaks from within us. Glory erupts from every pore. Pressure applied produces diamonds. Many facets of fruit are without measure because when Jesus fully matures inside, He's all that is left. We are simply shells. We should remain calm, compassionate, and joyful when provoked. We only exhale His breath, leaving a glory trail as we walk the narrow path into eternity.

In the mature sons and daughters, all that is seen is the Glory of God shining through our earthly vessels, and we rise as a multitude of Jesuses multiplied on the Earth. Perhaps when His eyes rise to match our eyes, it is the fulfillment of seeing Him face to face, as the scriptures reference. How many would make room for Him to grow, knowing that one day they would look in the mirror and see the eyes of Jesus staring back at them?

 PAUSE

I feel led to share a bit about my testimony and the ways I hear the voice of God. It's hard to decide where to start, but my first solid memory of encountering God's voice was around four. We lived at my grandpa's house, and as I played in the backyard, I climbed into my tree house and heard an audible voice call my name. At the moment, I felt a bit like Samuel with his first encounter with the voice of God. All I heard was my name, "SARA." I searched and looked for the person who had called my name. I went inside and asked my mom if she had called me. Although the voice was thunderous, I didn't have any reference to who could have called my name. I didn't know for many years that it was, in fact, the voice of God. I also never forgot that moment. I was sharing the story with a friend, and she spoke about what I had wondered about and confirmed God could speak in an audible voice, even in our generation. I haven't received God's words audibly since that day, but I know he can do it. There is NOTHING he cannot do. For most of my childhood and early adult life, I knew God was speaking to me, but I didn't have a background in the spirit-filled community to teach me or show me how to listen. It wasn't until a few years ago that I started to HEAR clearly and discern the voice of God.

One way I describe how I have experienced God's voice is like downloads, a surge that washes over you suddenly. For example, there have been moments when I'm seeking the Lord, and I suddenly turn a corner or walk into a different room, and "Boom," a transmission of revelation and understanding is dropped into my spirit. It pierces your spirit like osmosis to your heart, a form of communication without an audible voice. I want you to know that you shouldn't expect it to always seem clear. Sometimes, the enemy brings confusion and fog to intercept God's voice. It doesn't necessarily mean there is anything you have done to change his voice. I want to encourage people by saying I don't always feel or hear with complete clarity but regularly and intermittently, and not always using the same method. God speaks to us in many creative ways and always tries to teach us new ones. It's like learning a new Language. The first clear, undeniable words are sometimes spoken to place a fire and create a desire and a hunger to know Him more. I desire to increase the frequency until it's no longer intermittent and sporadic but a constant clear flow.

Let's pause and pray a few short prayers from my journal together.

Holy Spirit,

Lead me with a loud voice so I know when to pause and when to go.

Lead me and teach me your ways.

Direct my path like Phillip and Peter and let it be clear and loud.

In Jesus' Name,

Amen.

Scripture Reference

Deuteronomy 33

Lord,

Teach us to follow in Your steps and accept Your teaching. Let us live and not die, bringing unity to Your Kingdom. Give us strength to advance Your Kingdom and defend us from Your enemies. Let us obey Your Word and guard Your covenant. Accept the work of our hands as an offering as You increase our ministry. Bless our land and enlarge our territory to the west and the south. Let us prosper in our travel and in our time at home. Secure our boundaries and hold us in Your everlasting arms. Be our shield and our sword.

In Jesus' Name,

Amen.

A Prayer for Discernment

Scripture References

1 Kings 3:9-14; 2 Samuel 14:17,20; 1 King 7:40; 2

Samuel 23:2; 1 Kings 6:18; 2 King 10:31

Lord,

Grant me an understanding heart so I can know the difference between right and wrong. Help me navigate through the place I am planted and all the dark places You send me. Let me learn from the mistakes of Jehu and follow the Lord, the God of Israel, with my whole heart. Destroy every idol on my path, not keeping one. Every lie and idol must go. Please show me the lies and idols and instruct me in Your strategy to remove each. Teach me to be like the angels of God to discern quickly and easily what isn't from You. Help me separate the words spoken from the vessel to process situations and respond in the correct action, word, and deed. In every moment, let the Holy Spirit speak through me as the words of the Father rest on my tongue.

Allow me to be like Huram and complete all of my assignments from the King. Let me complete them with beauty, attentiveness to every detail, and quality artistry and skill that make each piece strong from top materials that endure.

Thank you for a sanctuary decorated with flowers in full bloom.

In Jesus' Name,

Amen.

Let's look at some of my journal notes that may help you discern people and situations.

Scripture References

1 Corinthians 15:55-56, Ezekiel 37:5

Testing Fruit

When you look for flesh in the flesh, you will find and see it.

When you open your eyes and look through the veil, you will see the heart motive in the spirit.

Look for the fruit on the tree; when you find it, you will know if it is bitter or sweet.

The tree is dead if you do not find fruit on the tree. Fortunately, bringing dead things back to life is kingdom work. It's not too late to receive a new life.

It's time for a drink of living water through the baptism of the Holy Spirit, which has the resurrection power to raise the dead to life. He will breathe into you once more.

Scripture Reference

Psalm 51:15

Father,

We are thirsty and hungry. Please do not abandon us. Open up rivers and give us fountains of water in our valleys. Fill our desert with pools of water.

We are hungry and desperate for You. You promised if we seek You, we will find You. Father, I desire more of You and Your Kingdom, so I call forth rivers of Your Holy Spirit pouring into fountains in our churches and living temples. Fill the dry, barren, empty buildings with pools of water to immerse the dry, thirsty, and hungry people.

Help me to cry out like a woman in labor interceding with You. Let us not praise ourselves but burn off all pride and arrogance disguised as godly confidence. Let the reverse be true as well. Let the boldness of the Lord be recognized as it is and not be mistaken for arrogance and pride. Let Your truth be made known in the hearts of man. Let us reflect Your glory, Lord.

Unseal our lips so that we might praise You.

In Jesus' Name,

Amen.

Chapter 1 Journal Notes

SARA C GEORGE

CHAPTER 2

RISE UP, TAKE YOUR POSITION

Every time we circle Yahweh just as the Earth circles the sun, seasons change, revealing a new part of who we are in him. We reflect what we watch and identify with. If we keep our eyes focused on Jesus, looking at him and his glory, we will start to assimilate him and reflect his glory here on Earth right where we are planted.

*For all creation is waiting eagerly for that future day when God will reveal who his children really are. - **Romans 8:19 NLT***

There is a supernatural realm. It's wonderous to explore. When given a glimpse of its existence it gives us room to dream and explore like in the days of our childhood. What are your dreams? What are your answers to the childhood question of what you want to be when you grow up? Do you remember? Perhaps in the graciousness of our Father, He is opening doors, granting dreams, and answering prayers.

Don't be afraid to dream. Stop for a moment, consider the ponderings of your childhood, and answer those questions for yourself. What did you enjoy? How did you pass the time and seasons? I will tell you some things I experienced in my childhood that I am beginning to connect to God and understand the way He was drawing and pursuing me even as a child of the 80s. I tell you these stories not to elevate myself but instead to invite you to remember your youth so that you might be stirred by memories of your childhood to see the hand of God present and holding you day by day.

As a teen, I wrote in my journal that I thought I would become a missionary, not overseas, but right here in the USA. It seems that without striving, I can see how the Lord has directed my path in the last few years. I can see the fulfillment of the word as I write. Writing was a pastime of my youth. I would just make up stories and songs. I didn't have the maturity to keep up with those things, but the joy it would bring me to go back and read them again would be immense. I was gifted in creative writing. I would frequently win certificates and accolades. I remember combining writing with pictures substituted for words. I enjoyed adding color to my writing and used these creative strategies to display my love for art. Now I can see it was training for interpreting dreams. Dreams are simply pictures that can be translated into words of knowledge or words of wisdom. The Lord has allowed me the privilege to partner with Him in translating dreams on occasion, which to me is incredible.

Coloring was my favorite pastime as a child. I loved the colors. I would sit for hours entertained by Crayola Crayons and my latest coloring books. As I got older, I took art lessons via television shows like Bob Ross. I loved listening to stories and using my imagination. I have fond memories of PBS, the public broadcasting station that encouraged and inspired me with content to further my imagination through reading, writing, and exploring. My favorites were "Reading Rainbow," "Sesame Street," "Captain Kangaroo," "Mr. Rogers," and those telethon movie series for fundraising, "Anne of Green Gables," a young author and hopeless romantic.

I led peers in worship after having experienced praise and worship on a youth mission encounter. I have memories of taking walks alone and singing praise and worship music. I haven't ever pursued music in any form, but as I am typing, I contemplate this very idea or thought, wondering if the Lord has any blueprints for my life involving music. I suppose we are all on a "as need to know" basis and I just don't know the answer to that pondering just yet. I hope you pause just a moment and let the Holy Spirit remind you of your childhood.

What if all of these things were there to plant seeds into my life to give me a foundation to grow? This is why it's important to look back and remember who you were as a child before you were crushed by the world. What were your natural interests and inclinations? I encourage you to journal and remember who you were because it will lead you back to who you were created to become.

There was a season during my transformation when I often anointed myself as I left my home each day and started praying for the Holy Spirit to be my teacher and guide. I was inviting the Holy Spirit to give me my identity in Christ through this process. I would anoint my forehead using a small cross pattern, my eyes to see what God desires me to see, my ears to hear the voice of God, my temples to receive the mind of Christ, my lips and even my throat to be the voice of God, my hands to do His work, and my feet to go where God desires to lead me.

No human told me to do this. It was just something I felt led in my spirit to do. This process of walking on the path God has for you will fast track you into your identity God created you to fulfill. Interestingly, I remember being surprised when he started to answer my prayers.

 **PAUSE**

The process of anointing is a reminder to pray to ask for God's protection and guidance daily. It is not to be confused as some type of ritual or superstition – the oil itself was a reminder for me because it was and is my heart's posture to be led by the Spirit of God.

Let me explain how and why I started anointing myself. Tia, a friend of mine, had a season of life where she would sign messages with a catchphrase, "Blessed and Anointed." I was curious and wanted to understand what it meant. The phrases Blessed and Anointed are words of identification. They describe who we are spiritually. I didn't yet discern I was seeking my identity, but it was time for me to wake up from slumber. I had heard the term blessed and had thought I knew what it meant; however, looking back, I really didn't have a firm grasp on what blessed meant. My friend explained that she had been raised by her grandmother, and her grandmother had taught her to anoint her home and family with oil. I wanted to understand how she used it and what she did, so I asked her if she would anoint my house. She came one day and prayed with me over my house and showed me how to anoint doorways and pray over rooms. In case you are starting from the position I was in at this point, let me explain a bit about what we did. She brought olive oil and prayed for the protection of God to be represented in the oil. Oil is representative of the Holy Spirit.

At this point, I didn't know anything about that part. I did connect the dots that it was similar to the representation of the Passover when the Jews were instructed to paint the blood of a lamb over the entry into their homes so the death angel would pass over them. I began to read more about how the shepherds used oil on their lambs' heads as a protectant. It can protect the skin, and it protects the herds. It would make sense that the Holy Spirit would create a barrier of protection over homes and people. I felt compelled to carry out the tradition passed from my friend's grandmother. I sought the Lord and grew in knowledge of the Word of God through the Holy Spirit. The biblical teaching for anointing was highlighted as I continued to practice anointing. There are many scriptures about anointing in the Bible. Recently I was reading Exodus and discovered the Scripture that correlates to anointing your home. It is an example of Moses anointing the Tabernacle. Exodus 40:9

 UNPAUSE

Who am I? This is a question of identity. As I grow in the Lord, I'm discovering our individual lives are created to carry many character traits and positions depending on our surroundings and seasons. Every time we circle Yahweh just as the Earth circles the sun, seasons change, revealing a new part of who we are in Him. We reflect what we watch and identify with. If we keep our eyes focused on Jesus, looking at Him and His glory, we will start to assimilate Him and reflect His glory here on Earth right where we are planted. He is like a diamond, like a jewel with many facets and colors. Let's reflect Him in every color and come into agreement with his creativity. There is a season of creativity pouring out on the Earth in this hour to do something new and different to bring in the harvest at this moment in time.

In certain stages of life, when we are trying to discover who we are, we often try various types of friend groups to see where we fit in and feel accepted. We tend to transform in these conditions. Over time, these cliques of people start to seem similar, almost as if they are one person. When we find ourselves not listening and looking at Jesus sometimes, we take on the wrong identity. It seems we all reach a place of reset in our lives that we need to stop and ask ourselves "Who am I to God? Who was I created to be? What is my destiny, my purpose?"

I'm still discovering who God says I am. I asked him once, "Who am I to you God?" He answered me. He clearly and passionately told me. He spoke to me in a rush, downloading into me like osmosis to my heart. It wasn't audible, but it was undeniable. When He opened my scroll and read my position in the Kingdom of God, it was a life-changing moment. I was flooded with a sense of urgency for the Kingdom of God and knew there was nothing more important than fulfilling my role to bring people into God's Kingdom. I have had a couple of visions, but the most three-dimensional encounter happened when He opened my scroll and read my position. This encounter I can only describe as an out-of-body experience. It reminds me of those near-death experiences people talk about. I was physically in one place but supernaturally transported at the moment somewhere completely different.

I watched the scene take place as if I were there, and it was much more real than a dream. I felt excitement mixed with freedom as I was being baptized in a lake of blood. It did not repulse me in any way. Even though I am a bit queasy and uneasy with injury and bodily fluids, I was at perfect peace, and no fear was present. I understood that it was the blood of Yeshua. There aren't words to describe what my spirit was receiving. It's as if, spiritually there are more than five senses, and my physical body cannot comprehend and translate it fully. It's as if the English language doesn't have a word to capture the emotion. The best I can do to describe the moment is the word FREEDOM. It was as vivid as if I had physically been there. I saw my hair wet and flying in the movement, and I saw the light and felt a surge of refreshing, exhilarating renewal with empowering energy.

⏸ PAUSE

I didn't always know what it meant when someone said they had a vision. Do you know? It's a considerably basic concept, but nevertheless, depending on your spiritual and religious background you may not understand the concept.

The first personal experience I had with someone having a vision was my friend Pam who told me as we prayed, she pictured us at the foot of the cross. I didn't know a vision could be a simple image of the supernatural in the natural. I have heard of different types of visions and some people seem to have very three-dimensional visions. Most of mine have been considerably basic and very infrequent in occurrence up to this point. In my realm of understanding, a vision is simply an image popping up in your mind, almost like a movie screen or a dream. You can identify it based on the fact that it wasn't anything you were thinking, and it just dropped into your mind's eye or the imagination part of your brain.

 UNPAUSE

God has many things in store for those who seek Him. I encourage you to start pondering your position in the heavenly realm. Ask Abba the question like I did. Ask Him, "Who am I to you?" In His perfect timing, He will answer your request. I grabbed the nearest piece of scratch paper and a pen and wrote down all that he told me. He shared things I never knew I would witness, let alone be a vessel on this earth for Him to move in that way.

Do not allow fear to grip you or stop you from the assignments God has given to you. Fear does not come from God, and it cannot contain the glory the Lord has prepared. It must be removed as Jesus grows within us. In fact, the only power fear has is intimidation. Fear is a prison, building supernatural boundaries and walls. It chains us down as slaves to the world, but it's time we reconcile the strength God placed in us at conception.

Realize this world is not our home. We are citizens of Heaven, a kingdom, not of this world. It's time to see ourselves like Samson, pulling down the walls and pillars of every lie that taught us to live in fear. Consider that it is not God who gives fear. In fact, fear is taught by the liar himself. Fear is a strategy from hell.

Throughout our lives, from the earliest moments, the enemy sends assignments to teach us how to be afraid and why we should assemble walls of imprisonment. It's time to recognize that it has shaped our culture and society, altering our original design. Once we can start to recognize the thought patterns and teachings that were passed down from a seed of fear, we can tear down the walls brick by brick. Peace and a sound mind are our inheritance from Heaven. Heaven is releasing strategies to remove Satan's roots in our lives. Let us start by pulling out fear from its roots.

I pray that anyone who is reading these words will be enlightened by the Holy Spirit, who is the Revealer of all truth and The One who opens blind eyes. May this be more than words on a page, but instead a seed that inspires change and transformation within many lives, breaking away the darkness and bringing us closer to the light of Jesus Christ. Visualize Christ beside you as you read. If you have accepted Him as your Lord and Savior, He is always there. If you recognize that you have not surrendered your life to Him, take this moment to cry out to Him and ask Jesus to join you in this journey, revealing Himself through these pages. Let this be an appointed time in your life to encounter His love, light, and truth. Jesus Christ has risen, so take Him out of the neat little church walls and allow Him to sit beside you. Church boundaries have made Christians too complacent by allowing a spirit of religion to influence our minds instead of allowing the Holy Spirit to influence our hearts. Wherever two or more gather in His name, He is there and present. Let us become one as the Christian body unites, removing the veil and going deeper together. He will take your hand and walk you into the fire towards the light of the living Kingdom. Allow the Holy Spirit to direct your hands, feet, and voice. Ask yourself, "Why not me?" We will all be held accountable for our actions and inactions. Ask God to circumcise your heart and align your life with His blueprints. There is a harvest at hand and the workers are few. He is calling all believers to unite with a clear vision by the unification of the arising awakened remnant. He will unify us with His glory, and you can expect change to take place. There is only one heaven, and God's plan is for one church and one bride. It is time to stand together as we prepare for the Bridegroom. It's time to seek purity by removing every spot and wrinkle from your life.

 **PAUSE**

I need to pause and mention a revelation I received in Matthew 18:19-20. The power of agreement goes deeper, wider, and further than most of us understand. I believe the revelation I was given showed me this is a supernatural principle in heaven, a law of governing, so to speak. The opposite is also true. If two or more agree with Satan, he is given permission to react, assign, or harass through temptation, lies, and schemes, and that is why it is so important to bridle our tongues and avoid nodding and going along with idle gossip, slander, and negative words or false accusations being spoken over individuals. We have all found ourselves in those situations where we walk into a room, and someone wants us to agree with something they have just said, and it's usually a negative comment or slander. Out of fear of peers, many people go along with the gossip without speaking out, giving a defense, or pointing out the golden rule and treating people how we desire to be treated. The danger in this is it gives ammunition to the enemy to attack that person through our spoken words.

 UNPAUSE

Let us pray for a blessing of identity and purpose to come alive in each believer together.

Scripture References

Luke 1:37,38, 45; Luke 2:9,14

The Christmas Blessing

Let the radiance of the Lord's Glory surround me.

Glory to God in the highest heaven and peace on Earth to those with whom God is pleased.

I please the Lord, and I am the Lord's servant.

May everything, He says about me come true.

I am blessed because I believe that the Lord will do what He says.

For the Word of the Lord God will never fail.

In Jesus' Name,

Amen.

Let's pray this simple prayer from my journal.

Scripture References

Romans 2:29, Psalm 119

A Key to Turn Hearts

Make me a true Jew, Lord, seeking praise from God and not people. Lord, You lead the ones You redeem with Your unfailing love. As Your beloved redeemed bride, I seek understanding, guidance, and clarity with detailed instructions like Paul, Moses, and Noah. Align us for Your purpose and plan. Give me a heart like David. Let my mind be as Christ's mind in perfect working order, removing any and all genetic curses and mutations in my DNA, cleansing my body at the cellular level, detoxifying each cell, and bringing it into the wholeness and perfection as You created them within Your original design before the corruption of sin entered the world.

In Jesus' Name,

Amen.

Chapter 2 Journal Notes

_____

_____

_____

_____

_____

_____

_____

_____

_____

_____

_____

_____

_____

_____

_____

_____

_____

_____

_____

_____

_____

_____

_____

_____

_____

_____

_____

_____

_____

CHAPTER 3

JUST A LITTLE MUSTARD SEED

A good place to start "Looking for Tiffany" is to pray that God will increase your FAITH.

Forgiveness and repentance lead the way for growth into a new creation. It makes room to grow by removing hard stones that block new roots.

"Send out your light and your truth; let them guide me. Let them lead me to your holy mountain, to the place where you live." -Psalm 43:3 NLT

"You don't have enough faith," Jesus told them. "I tell you the truth, if you had faith even as small as a mustard seed, you could say to this mountain, 'Move from here to there,' and it would move. Nothing would be impossible."

Matthew 17:20 NLT

Lord,

Let us be the generation to move mountains. Bless us with mustard seed faith.

Amen.

 **PAUSE**

Let's pause and pray together this simple prayer from my journal.

Thank you, Heavenly Father, for Your abundant blessing in my life. Every day I open my eyes, I am grateful and blessed. I want to follow Your path. I believe, but forgive my unbelief. We think we have faith, but if we only believed as much as a mustard seed, there would be so much more. Guide me, Father. Give me wisdom and direct my feet so they stay on solid ground. Light my way with more than a lamp. I need beams of light like an airstrip to guide my way. Allow me to show Your love and be Your hands and feet on Earth.

Increase my faith and mark our generation with mustard seed faith. Increase our faith through the encouragement found in these testimonies. Release assignments that will bring a new level of faith. Teach us to trust You as we obey step by step.

In Jesus' Name,

Amen.

 **UNPAUSE**

I wasn't always looking for Tiffany in my life. First, God had to wake me up and get my attention. Journey with me as I tell you how the Holy Spirit pursued me. He chose me and ordered my steps long before I had fully surrendered. He desired to take my faith to the next level and knew I would retrace the path I crossed and see His faithfulness in the details. It's like watching a movie about your life when you can catch the revelation of God's intricate plan.

In 1999, I was searching for my first home as a new college graduate. I was living my life second-guessing the principles I had been taught as a child. I believed the lies that justified my decisions. I was overconfident and ready to fly without realizing I didn't have wings yet. Not wanting to live in an apartment building, I bought a beautiful mountaintop property. It was raw, undeveloped land. Perhaps that's how God saw me in this phase of life. I was raw and undeveloped. It was a home for a pioneer. There wasn't a road or a telephone line when I made the purchase. It was quite an adventure with beauty and frustration. A place for personal growth and new understanding.

As seasons changed in a few short years, my husband and I found ourselves in new circumstances with a toddler and a second baby on the way. We decided it would make more sense to move into a developed area with fenced-in spaces to accommodate toddlers.

Fifteen years after the move, my daughter and I drove back one Sunday afternoon to see where our family began. The Holy Spirit enlightened me, and in my current state of living a life in the transformation of the heavenly realm, I could see and understand the prophetic details of my life. Without understanding and intention when I purchased this mountain property, I simply stumbled across a development in which the owner saw fit to name the streets from the Bible. The property I purchased was on the corner of Jericho and Promise Land Drive. Our address was 105 Jericho Road. Even more intriguing is the fact that the new owner told me that, over the years, the property had been assigned a new address. This specific corner lot had been reidentified, and it goes by a new name. It is no longer Jericho Road, but instead Promise Land Drive.

The revelation I was given just makes my spirit do cartwheels. I love cartwheels! You see, in that season of life, I was living in Jericho, the old town, before the walls fell down. After the baptism of the Holy Spirit and Fire, I am a new creation being transformed into the likeness of Christ. The darkness is being removed to reveal the truth. It was as if an angelic army had taken down all of my walls and set me free. I am free to live in the Promised Land. What great detail our Father went into coordinating my address, knowing the exact date He would take me back to physically cross over onto 'Promise Land.' He knew at this point in my maturity, I would be looking and searching for Him in the details, and He would be glorified in the mystery unveiled. You see, that's the Living God, the one I serve, who cares to know my street address and coordinates the numbers to a scripture verse given to me in 2020. For me, 105 Jericho equals Joshua 1:05 or 1:5.

*"No one will be able to stand against you as long as you live. For I will be with you as I was with Moses. I will not fail or abandon you." - **Joshua 1:5 NLT***

What glorious encouragement from the one who lifts my head.

 PAUSE

A memory of a divine encounter that I want to share involves an answered prayer that increased my faith. I was in church one Sunday morning and prayed that God would use me specifically on that day. My family went to a local theme park, and spontaneously, my husband was fidgety and ready to leave.

I tried to talk him into staying longer, but he refused, so we headed home. Suddenly, on this beautiful afternoon, we drove into a rain shower. Both of our children fell asleep in the car, which was unusual because it was a short ride, and it just didn't normally happen that both kids would be asleep at the same time on a car ride. Nevertheless, simultaneously, both fell into a deep sleep on the drive home. Out of the corner of his eye, my husband saw a motorcycle going in the opposite direction flip on the slick road. If we had left two minutes earlier, we would never have noticed the accident. If we had left five minutes later, we would have been in traffic on the opposite side as it was at a complete standstill awaiting a med flight helicopter. We circled around to the scene of the accident, and as we got out to assist, all we could hear was the wailing of a man I now know as "Tiger." Two or three other cars pulled over to assist as well.

My husband was calm enough to remember the CPR training we received when I was pregnant with our first child. He administered CPR to the wife, who was lying down on the asphalt. I was calm and able to ask questions and make phone calls for the husband. I asked him if he had children, if the woman had any children, and who we could contact for him as her next of kin. I dialed the numbers for him and spoke to his mother. There were a couple of other eyewitnesses who also pulled up to respond. Together, we joined in unity to aid the family. Two or three of us held hands and prayed with the man on the scene. The ambulance arrived, and the paramedics went to my husband's side to take over the CPR and emergency medical treatment. The emergency medical team called in a Medi-flight helicopter and fought to get a pulse. As the emergency team left and the police drove the husband, who was not injured, to the hospital, my family continued home.

During this ordeal, neither of my children woke. My husband told me that the wife would not survive because he had felt her spirit go with her last breath as he administered CPR. We decided that we should go to the hospital to check on this man, who we knew was alone dealing with the sudden death of his spouse. My mother-in-law was able to make herself available and drive from about 45 minutes away to watch our young kids. I remember getting a shower and even grabbing a James Dobson book I had purchased months earlier titled, "When God Doesn't Make Sense." We drove the thirty minutes to the hospital emergency room to see if, by chance, we had made it in time to be of some assistance. I walked over to the desk to ask about the couple, and as I spoke to the nurse, the on-staff minister walked out a side door with our new friend. He had just told him his wife did not make it through. We were there at the exact moment to walk to him and sit with him while he waited to see his wife one last time. He told us his story and travel plans. Jesus was able to use us as an extension of His hands and feet as we made sure he had everything he needed to make it through the night. A friend of his was flying in the next morning to trailer his motorcycle and drive him back home. We shared the circumstances with the hotel attendant, and we discovered later that the hotel had given him a complimentary room. As time passed, we stayed friends, and he shared all the discoveries of how God had been working and preparing his wife. I have heard of this from time to time, that sometimes people seem to just know when days are drawing near. It was a tragic event, but God was still present and proving Himself faithful every step and moment. In time, we celebrated his next season of life with a second bride and bonus sons for a new beginning. We remain friends to this day. This encounter was an incredible example of God's perfect timing.

 UNPAUSE

Let's continue looking back at the journey that brought a transformation, increasing my faith along the way. The beginning of transformation requires a recognition of the need for cleansing. Forgiveness and repentance led the way for me to grow into a new creation in Christ Jesus. In the second half of 2018, I felt the Holy Spirit stir my heart to clear up some of the unforgiveness and bitterness that had been growing in my heart's garden. I didn't understand how much it affected my walk with God. My friend John called me early one morning out of the blue. At this time, we were only acquaintances, but I knew he was a man of God. He spoke to me and gave me some Scriptures. Shortly after that, I clearly received instructions or an assignment from God to make amends with specific family and friends. I was instructed to get up the next day and drive over in person to visit with each one. I went to see my friend Tia and asked for prayer in my efforts and journey. Her family gathered with me in a circle to pray. I was forgiven that day and started to understand how important it is to forgive and allow the Holy Spirit to remove the emotional response to past offenses and trauma. Harboring ill feelings, resentment, and offense blocks our prayers and prevents God's Kingdom from manifesting, as He desires within our lives. This day was just the first and most immediate layer of unforgiveness I needed to remove from my life. In my growth, I can see now that it will continue until every old situation in our lives has become new and redeemed by the blood of Christ as He has forgiven us and died as our Sacrificial Lamb and example.

Shortly after the forgiveness drive took place, one morning, I pulled up to my office in November 2018. I was overwhelmed by the Holy Spirit to write as I listened to a download of truth that was bringing healing and untwisting my twisted thoughts.

 PAUSE

Let's pause and review my notes from that morning.

I serve a Mighty King and His Son, Jesus Christ. He has revealed a bit of wisdom to me this morning.

Children come into this world with complete trust and pure love for those around them. We are told our relatives love us. It is an unquestioned fact. It comes as a great shock when those closest to us start to act in ways that show they are living in a compromised world. We expect our closest friends and family to hold to a higher standard than the world. When compromise comes as a surprise, it wounds our hearts. Heart wounds are like big rocks and tree roots in the soil of a garden. They make it hard to till and hard for new growth to take root. As we carry heart wounds, we become jaded, insecure, and scared. We let fear build thick walls around our hearts (garden), and we guard the gates.

This is a strategy, an elaborate scheme designed by an enemy to steal joy and peace. It holds us back from fulfilling the life God has written for us. This place we live in Satan has been cast into, and we do not live alone in it as some might think. We are foolish thinking our thoughts all belong to us. The enemy whispers what our flesh wants to hear. If we are not dressed in our spiritual armor and prepared for this mirage of sweet and attractive thoughts, we become easy prey, allowing him to kill, steal, and destroy our destiny.

Satan wants to put us in chains. His goal is to bind up every believer to keep us from taking our positions doing the work of the Father. We cannot stand when we are in shackles and chains. They are too heavy for us to rise into formation. Satan has limited power, so he goes fishing, waiting for us to bite the bait and hook. When we start to agree with his lies, he hands us the chains of unforgiveness, offense, and bitterness. We chain ourselves, pulling them on and turning the lock, which is the wall of "Safety" we live inside.

Then, one day, Jesus walks into the room, wakes us up, and opens our minds to see the scheme and we can see Jesus holds the key to take off every chain.

If you are holding onto offense and bitterness and not freely forgiving the way you have been forgiven, God cannot reach down and unwrap the chains until you let go by forgiving. Stop death gripping the chain; instead, let the Holy Spirit help you repent and forgive, allowing God to pull off the chains and shackles.

Ask God to separate the actions and hurts from the person so you can see the hand of the enemy unveiled. Forgive and Move Forward, leaving the past behind you and God's face before you.

We are often far too burdened and heavy with chains. Recognize that the enemy's victory is temporary. Lighten your load in obedience to the Father by letting go and letting forgiveness in your life tear down the walls and remove the heavy chains. God wants to move mountains. You better lighten your load so that you can stand and lift your own corner of that mountain.

Additional Journal Notes on Conflict and Forgiveness

Scripture References

1 Corinthians 4:12-13, 2 Corinthians 7:8-9, 11

Romans 12:20, Proverbs 21:14, Luke 6:27-29

To bless your "enemy" allows God to legally come to your defense by completely rendering you blameless after you have repented and blessed others involved.

By blessing the ones, you have held offense, bitterness, and unforgiveness towards, I feel it takes forgiveness to the next level. When you can bless someone, you will know if you truly have let go of the burden. Blessing not only the ones you have harbored these feelings towards, but also the ones who may be holding anger or offense towards you changes everything.

It frees you in the spirit so God can move on your behalf. He changes your heart, and you will know that you have forgiven when you can enjoy giving them a gift or blessing without feeling angst or offense towards them. Often, words without action are void or are done out of intellect and not the right heart motive. When we go the extra step and bless those who do us harm, I see that it changes us on the inside and helps us to truly let go, removing any intentional or unintentional wrong we may have caused. It completely sets us free so that God can defend us and work on our behalf.

Look to the Holy Spirit to provide you with creative strategies to bless the ones who hold offense towards you or may have spoken in slander or gossip unintentionally or intentionally, casting a curse against you. Pray and ask the Holy Spirit to reveal the ones who have charges against you.

 UNPAUSE

As the soil in my heart now had room for new seeds to take root, I started taking notice of my friend John testifying of miracles daily in his surf shop. I pondered and considered his testimonies. I had known John for several years. I knew him personally, so I couldn't dismiss what he was experiencing. I knew him well enough to believe he was being truthful. Up to this point, my knowledge of the Bible was from attending the local Baptist Church. Every time the doors were open, my family attended. I went to vacation Bible school and church camp in the summer. I was raised in church, and I had never heard of modern-day miracles happening on a daily basis like this man was testifying about. I searched my memory for what I knew about the subject and could only recall how, when the question about God performing miracles in the present day was asked of teachers or pastors, the responses differed from person to person and were answered more from each one's personal opinion. I did go on a teen mission trip one year in which I believe we encountered miracles, but I wasn't certain because of the language barrier. I had not considered the same kinds of things could be possible at home. However, this was the seed in my memory bank I was looking for, and now it was time for God to water it. I needed to study for myself and decide what I believed. I started reading about spiritual gifts in 1 Corinthians. The Holy Spirit overwhelmed me, and, in a moment, while sitting in my car, I had this download of unspoken words that pierced my heart. I knew my answer. God can do miracles, and they aren't confined to the days of the Bible! The revelation and sudden understanding felt like it opened a door to a hidden world. The awakening of my spirit had begun. In the fall of 2019, I became a firsthand witness to a healing miracle.

My friend Brittany announced a Sunday night book study on the prophet Elijah. I knew internally that my answer should be "yes." The group who met together was unlike any other group of women I had met up to that point. We were called there for a purpose. During the course of this season, I started to gain boldness and offered to speak in front of the group on occasion. My faith was building. The same friend hosting the Bible study hosted a fundraiser for a mission trip to Peru one weekend. It was a drop-in event on a Sunday afternoon. Randomly, after lunch, I decided it was time to head over to the event. I had a divine appointment that led to a prayer for a teen girl to receive salvation and healing in her eyes. There were several tabletop vendors and stations. As I walked around and visited different booths, I heard a young girl talk about having trouble with her vision. She brought up her problem with sight out of context, which raised a flag in my spirit. I thought to myself, "That's a bit odd." She had one eye that she described as completely black or "blind" and one fuzzy eye.

Pay attention to the random things you hear and look for clues. I had been anointing myself and specifically praying that I would hear what my Father hears and see what my Father sees. I went over to talk to my friend who was hosting the fundraiser, and she encouraged me to step out and offer to pray for healing. I walked over to the young girl and asked if I could pray for her eyes. She immediately started to get teary and agreed to prayer. I anointed her and began to pray. As I spoke, I started to prophesy over her life and asked for healing. When I finished the prayer, I asked her if she could see, and there had not been any change. I said something wasn't right and felt compelled to ask her about salvation in Jesus. She responded with nodding and more tears, and I prayed with her for receiving Jesus Christ into her life. Then I told her we would now pray again for her eyes. She asked if my friend could join us, and when I went to ask her, she announced that everyone present would join together to pray for this girl's sight to return. We all prayed simultaneously for her miracle. Everyone went back to what they had been doing before the prayer, and as I continued to stand with the girl, I asked her to check her eyes. She went to the bathroom, washed her face, and returned, saying that the fuzzy eye was now clear and that the light had returned to her dark eye. I was so excited and honored at that moment to witness firsthand an undeniable miracle. The girl's grandmother returned to pick her up, and I was blessed to be present when she told her that Jesus had healed her. What an honor and blessing. So much excitement filled me from the inside out. I had the confirmation I needed to increase my faith that miracles would happen when Jesus walked into a room.

As I began to seek God and come to some new understanding, it transformed my life. I realized that I needed to study and read the Bible for myself. I shouldn't rely solely on the beliefs and words of others to be my own. I discovered it isn't possible to have a relationship with someone without a personal pursuit through independent study and prayer. As the transformation began in my life, I realized that some "very good" people had taught me many things under the umbrella of "church," but if they didn't have their heart right when they were volunteering and teaching, what they taught could have been intertwined with tradition and personal opinions instead of divine flowing from the heart of God through his spirit. I discovered that it is possible to operate in the flesh of humanity through learned knowledge. The Holy Spirit also taught me that the words we speak are not always our own and can be compromised by the one who would steal, kill, destroy, confuse, and delay us from coming into alignment as heirs to the King. Revelation and new understanding had started to breakthrough and change how I think. It occurred to me that in the early church, things weren't taught in Sunday School. Instead, the new Christians and disciples were led by the Spirit of God.

The summer after I started anointing myself, I had another breakthrough. I went to Panama City Beach, Florida, for vacation. It was an unplanned trip. We wanted to go but did not have reservations. An opening became available one Sunday after church, so we packed up and left Sunday afternoon by about 3 p.m. While on vacation, we went to a public beach where I met a family who happened to be in ministry. They were different from many other "church people." I was drawn to them first by their family pet. I believe the dog's name was Fluffy. It was black and fluffy and floating on a raft in the ocean. It seemed unusual for a dog. I decided to approach them and ask questions. The response came from a voice with an accent I didn't recognize. My heart for other countries wanted to know more about where they were from and how they came to the United States. I first asked the basic mom questions, such as, "How old are your kids?" When she told me their names, I was intrigued further. The names were uncommon, so I asked how she came up with them. I was told stories of prophecy in the names. I think this was one of the first times I had ever heard about prophecy. She told me every time you speak your child's name, you are prophesying over their life. She also told me how she received a word of knowledge providing one of the children's names.

It was easy to see that this couple enjoyed body art, and I started to inquire about their tattoos. The tattoos were biblical and based on scriptures, which again caused me to engage in deeper conversation. I wanted to learn more, and the father told me he had a YouTube channel and had posted entire sermons on it about the meaning of his tattoos. I shared with this family about my friend John and how the ministry in his surf shop was thriving. I encouraged them to stop by as they went back through town.

Later that evening, I stopped by the Surf Shop as it was closing and asked John if he had met the family from South Africa. He said no, but someone called and left a message. He said it had been a full day, and he had not returned the call. I told him I would like to find the man's sermons and information, but due to the lack of pen and paper at the beach, I couldn't write it down. John just handed me the message with the phone number.

The next morning while in my quiet study time with the Lord, I sent a message asking about the YouTube channel. The minister, in turn, asked me to have John call him because he had something important to tell him. I told John he was waiting for him to call, and it was important. I then decided to get dressed and go on over to find out what it was all about. This was my first encounter with words of wisdom. I didn't fully understand, but John knew of the man's credentials, and he received an encouraging message about the increase in the healings and miracles to expect in his business. I was so excited to simply be a vessel for the connection because I knew it was God and not by chance that I was there that week in Florida and at that exact beach to meet this family. God is so good. When I returned home, I started to listen to the minister on YouTube, which stirred many more questions about my identity in Christ and the Holy Spirit.

After the beach encounter, watching the YouTube sermons, and listening to my friend John speak about a baptism of the Holy Spirit, I started to question if I could have received Holy Spirit baptism without understanding what it was. I started praying that God would baptize me in a way that I would no longer question that part of my identity in Him. I was told to find someone who prayed in tongues and ask them to pray for me to receive the baptism.

Unfortunately, I didn't know anyone who had that gift. When I told my friend John that I didn't know anyone who speaks in tongues, he told me to pray for the "Fire" in my quiet prayer time. I had no idea what John was talking about, but I did as instructed. I prayed for "The FIRE."

As I started to engage in conversations about the Holy Spirit, I discovered a friend had a daughter who spoke in tongues. As I asked more questions, she told me I was looking for a "Spirit-Filled" church. Unfortunately, when you look up listings of churches, they are not categorized, so someone searching can find a list of "Spirit Filled" churches. I asked her if she knew of any in our community, and she suggested one. I started praying about it and had been praying for months to meet the Holy Spirit through an official baptism of the Holy Spirit that would seal the questions in my heart, asking if I had ever been immersed in the Holy Spirit. My family decided to visit that "Spirit-Filled" church. We went a couple of times in the fall of 2019 and then started regularly attending in January 2020. In one of the first church services I attended, I heard someone give words of wisdom from the platform. During the first Wednesday night service I attended, they were doing a teaching series about the ministry of healing. I finally felt I had found a place to grow.

On a seemingly random Wednesday, visiting missionaries came to church and were invited to lead the service. At the end of the message, they invited people forward to pray for many things. I watched and considered if they might pray for my daughter and me for the baptism of the Holy Spirit. After the service, I found them and asked two couples, including the missionaries, to lay their hands on my daughter and me and pray for us to receive the Holy Spirit. I was able to look at my daughter and see something moving within her. I could feel a butterfly sensation and slight movement internally. My daughter started to speak in an unknown language, one she didn't know and was never taught. God had answered my petition in such a way that I could not continue to question whether or not I had been baptized in the Holy Ghost. However, I did not receive the gift of speaking in an unknown tongue that day.

Although I did not doubt, I had received the baptism of the Holy

Ghost, I continued over the next few months to seek an unknown tongue. I asked friends to pray for me to receive this prayer language at least three times in this interim period before I received it, which was approximately eleven months from the day my prayer was answered for an encounter of Holy Spirit Baptism.

In this season, I discovered a religious teaching that was trying to discourage and disarm me from pressing forward into the things of God. It is important to remember that the enemy is very good at catching us with our guard down by using a strategy of attack involving people in our inner circle whom we trust. Satan will attack any way he can wedge his way into our minds.

Some church doctrines teach that you cannot be baptized in the Holy Spirit and not speak in an "unknown" tongue. It is biblical evidence of Holy Spirit baptism. I agree it is a sign of Holy Spirit Baptism; however, in my personal experience and in others I have met not speaking in an unknown language is not a sign someone has not had a Holy Spirit Baptism. Based on my personal experience, I believe this is a common assumption that creates false teachings that have infiltrated some people's beliefs. If this is your belief, please do not be offended. Instead, be open to my personal testimony and use it as a conversation starter in your own communities by sharing your testimony and listening to others. I personally never doubted I had received the baptism. I really wanted to receive the gift of an "unknown" tongue and had not yet experienced it. I did experience a rapid increase in my spiritual fruit, including a strengthened prayer life. I was prophetically teaching in online videos and praying in the spirit using my native tongue. The misconception lies in this thought that it must be an "unknown tongue" to be spirit-filled. I often jokingly told people my spirit language must be English, but no one thought that was possible. In my opinion, it is a valid tongue. Many spirit-filled, tongue-talking Christians have experienced their individual prayer language spontaneously, changing between language types.

I kept pressing forward without concern. I prayed for people to receive the gift of tongues and the baptism of the Holy Spirit with the faith of a child. I witnessed the miracle. One day, several months later, someone I trusted told me I was not filled with the Holy Spirit because I did not speak in tongues. I was judged and made to feel that everything I was doing in the ministry for God was just inferior, cute, and a fruit of my childhood upbringing. These words broke my heart and crushed my spirit. I can interrupt this thought and say the person behind these words is an incredibly amazing friend of God whom I still admire to this day. It is not the person who hurt my feelings. It was the enemy coming to steal, kill, and destroy. He was simply using someone I trusted to try to push me off the course I was pursuing in my looking for Tiffany.

My relationship with Jesus was the most important part of MY life, and those words pierced my heart. I said, "I don't understand why you would say this to me." They tried to explain, while I sobbed, that I was doing something wrong and that it was somehow my fault because God freely gives this gift of tongues. Perhaps I didn't truly believe I could receive it for myself. At the moment, I didn't find these words comforting. Again, the person saying these words truly believed them and thought they were helping me somehow by explaining their beliefs. Perhaps it has helped someone in their life to hear this doctrine. It just wasn't helping me in that season of my life.

None of this made any sense to me at all. In fact, at this point, both of my children had received the gift of tongues before me. I was told it wasn't God withholding it; if it wasn't him, it was me, and I just didn't know how to receive it. I wailed, mourned, and considered what I had been told. After pondering the conversation, I realized what I was told lacked the comfort, peace, and love that is present when the Holy Spirit speaks. It was a word to hinder or halt my ministry from moving forward. Using discernment, it was easy to see it was an attack from the enemy seeking to silence my voice.

I want to add humility here and point out that in the Christian Walk throughout our lives, we can each look back and see moments in the past when we allowed the enemy to use us to hurt someone else through our words. I do not want to allow pride to fool me into thinking that I am not guilty of similarly being used by the wrong spirit. I pray that as I mature and grow in discernment with Christ, it happens less. The Bible warns us that the tongue speaks from both sides. The book of James 3:1-12 clearly describes the battle of the flesh we face. We tend to be offended and only remember the bad seeds someone plants during these types of mishaps, but over the course of this relationship there were many good seeds sown into the soil of my heart. I choose to remember and acknowledge all of the kindness and goodness I experienced in this relationship. Many seeds were planted in me that have been watered and produced fruit in my life and the lives of others. It's like the parable of the yeast: a little bit of yeast taints the whole batch. Most forget the good words spoken even though they outnumber the negative words. This is why it is so important to jump into the ocean and be cleansed from compromised thoughts and beliefs that would hinder others.

I believe a part of my assignment is to bridge the gap between the beliefs of non-spirit-filled churches and spirit-filled ones. Due to my experience, I can testify, warn, and encourage others who might encounter a similar religious spirit to keep pursuing Christ. I worked through my emotions, and in processing the offense, I chose not to be offended because God used this situation to uncover a false teaching. I was pushing and pursuing the gospel wholeheartedly, and I could not see where I could pursue my faith with any more vigor and intention than I was already doing. I evaluated my choices in this situation which clearly unveiled the enemy and his motives. Choice number one: I could give up. Choice number two: I could press forward without concern for anyone else's opinion. It is clear that my decision was choice number two because I knew without a shadow of a doubt that every message I recorded was received from the Lord. He was teaching and revealing himself so clearly. I could not deny him or my assignments.

The truth was clearly revealed, and with the encouragement of the Lord, I decided to keep going. Unfortunately, I have since had conversations with other people who believed God just didn't love or choose them because they felt like they were somehow unworthy of this special gift since they did not immediately pray in an unknown spirit language when baptized in the Holy Ghost. You may not agree with me or this logic, but I have been made victorious by the blood of the lamb, and my personal testimony cannot be taken from me. If you disagree with this portion of my testimony, check your heart for any offense, choose forgiveness and mercy for my testimony, and continue on this journey looking for Tiffany with me. In my opinion, the reason this belief has been handed down is for multiple reasons:

1. It is easier to prove the Holy Spirit baptism happened when an "unknown" tongue is the fruit of the baptism, but I might add my experience was not without fruit.

2. Often, the people who insist on this belief experienced an immediate gift of "unknown" tongues when they were baptized and do not want to consider the infinite creativity and methods of Yahweh, allowing for more than one method that contradicts their personal experience. Consider solving a math problem. Often, there is more than one way to solve the problem with the correct answer.

3. Many spirit-filled believers don't know how to explain the baptism outside of what they were taught handed down to them in oral tradition.

As the Holy Spirit compels you to seek and receive the Holy Spirit and Fire baptism, it is often given through impartation, ask a Holy Spirit-filled believer to lay hands on you and pray, asking God to use them as a conduit to impart his Holy Spirit and fill you. This is not the only way it happens. I have heard testimonials from people where the Holy Spirit came into a room without anyone laying hands. Pray and ask the Father to direct your path to receive Holy Spirit baptism.

 **PAUSE**

Let's pause and pray together this simple prayer from my journal.

Scripture References

Jeremiah 2:13, John 4:10-15, John 4:14

Additional Reference:

YouTube *Fountain of Living Water Sara George's Love Notes from Heaven:*
https://www.youtube.com/watch?v=04telnNq7nY

Father,

Fill me with your Holy Spirit so that I might not have to go draw water from the community well, but instead, make me a well for your waters to rise within me. I don't want to be a broken cistern requiring work to constantly refill. Seal every crack. Let not my well run dry but fill me with the ever-flowing fountain of you, the fountain of living water. Make me a bubbling, babbling spring. I surrender to you and your desires for me. I open my hands to receive any and all spiritual gifts you have wrapped and prepared for me. Lead me to encounter your Holy Spirit and Fire.

In Jesus' Name,

Amen.

Chapter 3 Journal Notes

SARA C GEORGE

CHAPTER 4

LOVE, A NATURAL RESOURCE

Love is the substance of all of creation. It's the very breath of life. It's what gives a heart its beat. It's the spark that ignites life.

"This is what the Lord says to the people of Judah and Jerusalem: "Plow up the hard ground of your hearts! Do not waste good seed among thorns.""

Jeremiah 4:3 NLT

"Plant the good seeds of righteousness, and you will harvest a crop of love. Plow up the hard ground of your hearts for now is the time to seek the Lord, that he may come and shower righteousness upon you."

- Hosea 10:12 NLT

"I have loved you even as the Father has loved me. Remain in my love."

- John 15:9 NLT

Let's talk about God's perfect love. Love is the substance of all of creation. It's the very breath of life. It's what gives a heart its beat. It's the spark that ignites life. Every cell in its original form was ignited into motion through love. Love is the only thing left when darkness is removed. It is the shining golden glory when we are removed from the fire.

The Father loves you and has not forgotten you. As sons and daughters, our Creator loves us deeply. He desires to hoist you up out of the sea as his buried sunken treasure. He will wash every piece of his treasure until it has a mirror shine to reflect Himself. Once you were lost, stolen, or sold by the pirates, but now he calls you found. You are hand-picked by Him. Each day in the life of one of God's chosen sons and daughters is an incredible love story. It just isn't until you reach a certain level of maturity that you begin to grasp the infinite love of our Heavenly Father. He is slowly and patiently pursuing you day by day.

In a vision, the Lord gave me a revelation of his love for us in a new way. Consider how on Earth we go and admire creation, natural wonders, national parks like the Grand Canyon, animals big to small, every one of them unique and admirable. We consider nature fun, refreshing, and beautiful. It's a place to go for vacation. I feel God sees us in the same way He goes to visit us and sees us from different angles and perspectives. Perhaps an analogy to explain what I'm trying to express is it's as if God has different glasses, like when we go to a 3D movie and put on special glasses, and we can see something that was previously hidden with our natural eye. He views us as wonders of the Earth. He admires each person and spends time gazing at each one. We can do something similar when going to view a world wonder like Niagara Falls. On the Canadian side of the falls, there are many attractions to seeing the falls from different perspectives. You can view from on top looking down, you can view from tunnel portals behind the falls, and you can view them from a boat and look up at the falls. We see the physical exterior in two-dimensional only. God sees the layers and beauty of every layer, organ, cell, and the beat of every heart. He sees every detail in full color. Sometimes, he goes to high points looking at his creations from a tower, and then sometimes, he chooses to experience us face to face, just like when we dive into the ocean. From every viewpoint, he admires us because he sees there is so much more than just our exterior. How deep is the love of a creator who chooses to admire us. Each one is a masterpiece in His hand.

God is simply waiting for his voice to be heard and recognized. He sends love notes to each one of us. We just need to sync with heaven. Synchronization allows us to receive and send love notes. It is heaven speaking and us listening.

There is more than one facet of love. Natural love or biological love can be observed between children and their parents or close biological relationships. You can love by practicing the characteristics of Christ day by day in our interactions that develop relationships of trust and mutual honor that turn to love with an element of time day by day and year by year. Then there is this whole other EXTRA kind of love that is completely supernatural and outside of ourselves. This is the Holy Spirit filling us with God's love for someone else. He will allow us to feel his emotions so we can partner with Him to love others well.

Love is patient and kind. Love is not jealous or boastful or proud or rude. It does not demand its own way. It is not irritable, and it keeps no record of being wronged. It does not rejoice about injustice but rejoices whenever the truth wins out. Love never gives up, never loses faith, is always hopeful, and endures through every circumstance. -1 Corinthians 13:4-7 NLT.

Our earthly definition of love, when examined in the Western world, looks quite different from God's words. The enemy whispers lies that hijack true love. If we go back to this passage whenever we are being fed lies by the enemy and compare the thought (lie) in question to God's definition of love, it might change our perspective. If we write down the lies and try to categorize what we are feeling on those down days, most likely, the feelings, thoughts, and actions we are judging are not God's definition of love. Love is not created. It simply exists. It isn't conditional based on your feelings, but it can be found when you look for the fruit of love. Where there is fruit, there is love. If the fruit is missing, pray for love to be drawn out of those around you. It was placed inside us at conception as an unlimited resource. We were divinely assembled with nothing missing, including a resource of love. Sometimes, we have to draw love out of others who don't have the tools or haven't been taught how to draw the love out. I see this visual aid of a well inside of us representing the resources we were gifted with at conception. Can you see it? It's deep in the ground with a rock ledge around it, a roof to keep it dry, and a pully lever system, but you have to bring your own bucket. Perhaps people around you are missing the indwelling conduit – "the bucket" – the Holy Spirit. Other people have experienced abuse and trauma, causing their "ropes" hearts to be cut or tangled, giving them a false idea or understanding of love. Pray that the Lord untangles the "rope" heart or replaces it with a brand new one.

The truth is most of us operate with compromised love on this side of heaven. We have moments of pure love, but it's difficult to draw from a well of love continually. It's as if there were two wells side by side, and if we are not consciously intentional and aware, we draw water on autopilot; sometimes, the bucket slips over into the wrong well, which happens to have leaks, leaving a very low water level and mud. The more we gain enlightenment about what love looks like, the easier it is to recognize when we serve muddy water from our buckets. Jesus said, "Remain in my love," so we must practice love. The good news is if you become aware and awake, you can catch your muddy water much quicker than if you are operating out of a zombie-like state. Mud is thick, and it can be caught in your hands; it's different from pure water that runs through your fingers.

Our goal should be to receive a revelation or understanding of truth that allows us to practice catching mud. Our aim should be to catch it before it is served. We may not hit the target every time, but with practice, you will begin to hit the mark more often. If we learn the definition of love, we can align with the truth in our circumstances and situations better.

Try meditating on the biblical meaning of love and inserting your name. You might even find it helpful to record it and play it back to yourself. Understanding can be gained through using multiple senses. Try finding creative ways to work through 1 Corinthians 13:4-7. Try speaking it, singing it, and even making funny accents when you speak. As you laugh through this exercise, try adding an element of smell. Maybe light a scented candle or spray a lovely perfume. Maybe write a song or play back the audio of the scripture as you paint or dance. The more senses you can combine to capture the revelation, the more it will help you catch and digest the fullness of the truth.

The enemy tries to convince us that love is conditional. Too often, we hear the phrase, "What do I get out of it?" The worldview of love is a self-seeking, self-centered view. In the Western world, we want to be pampered through our love language or personal definition of what love should be. It's often defined by physical intimacy and not consistency. The mark is missed in our mind's eye because we are looking for the culture's definition and not God's definition.

Acts of humility, patience, service, and honor often go unnoticed like a whisper. If you are not listening, you won't hear the whisper. If you are not measuring love by God's standards, you will easily miss it. Pure love can be compared to God's character and voice. It has fruit on the vine, and it pours out continually like a servant before others. It is the difference between a whisper and a loud siren. Culture's love is loud and makes you back away, which is actually the opposite of what we want. God speaks in a whisper so you will draw near.

If you don't see people drawing from the well of love, don't give up because love is patient with those around them. Love isn't in it to get something back. Love is a currency found in heaven. It makes you rich and opens doors. Love well, without measure. Don't hold back, but instead reflect your Father.

So now I am giving you a new commandment: Love each other. Just as I have loved you, you should love each other. Your love for one another will prove to the world that you are my disciples.   *-John 13:34-35 NLT*

In today's culture, we often replace love with codependency. In codependency, we see relationships for a season or convenience relationships that work to fill each other's voids. By the world's standard, it's accepted as love. In codependency, two people come to a relationship with holes wanting the other person to fill them – "You complete me," or you fill my void or momentary desire. This is not true love by a biblical definition. God's intended desire was for him to fill that God-shaped hole. Even though no one else can fill the void it doesn't stop us from trying. When two people who are filled with God become friends, there are no holes to fill. The need to be filled no longer exists. We love others based on drawing from an unlimited well of overflow or a high-water mark because we live in a place of intimacy with Christ.

When we are in a relationship with Christ, it's like rainfall filling the dry caverns in the ground. The longer you sit in the rain the more the soil is saturated, and every underground water source is filled. The well isn't shallow; it's deep and never goes dry.

 PAUSE

To avoid confusion and give clarity in this analogy I am no longer referring to the well as our resource of love, but instead using rain, water, and wells to represent intimacy of relationship with Christ, "Tiffany," the Presence of God, or Holy Spirit.

UNPAUSE

For the ones who do not have a personal relationship with Christ, they don't have a bucket and struggle to get a drink. The water level in their wells is low, not overflowing. They haven't experienced the rain filling empty caverns raising the water level. When they find a well in their desert not all of them are overflowing. Most require a bucket and lever system to draw water out.

In oasis areas, wells overflow. Let's compare an oasis to a conference or a worship service. In the overflow, anyone can come to the well, cup their hands, and receive a drink. During overflow, the thirsty must choose to cup their hands and drink. No one can force them to partake. They might get splashed with water or their feet wet, but they must be a partner with the well to be filled. Many people are constantly thirsty, wandering as if in a desert, and drawn into mirages that look like real fulfillment, but they are instead illusions of water. As they wander, panting and thirsty, they ask other people for a drink.

In the beginning, it is important to meet the immediate need of those around us by passing out water cups. By meeting this initial need it allows the thirsty ones time to focus on growing roots of understanding. It gives a window of opportunity to draw a map to the well while leading and teaching them the way to go to the source and draw water for themselves.

Sometimes, Christians get tired working to draw water for others. God isn't asking us to work hard passing out cups of water laboring in this way, but instead to partner with him. Sit in the rain until you are an overflowing well. Then it won't feel like a burden, and you won't grow tired. The ones who find themselves tired providing water cups do so for different reasons. Some people are trying hard because they want to feel needed and important. Other people only know how to draw water because it's what they have been taught and it's all they know how to do. For others it makes them feel good knowing and seeing needs fulfilled. To everyone around, watching people pass out cups of water looks like compassion and mercy, but over time, it becomes enabling. God doesn't want us to enable others by being their supply and only source of living water.

Don't grow tired and weary serving the thirsty. Instead of continuing to provide water, teach people how to use their own spiritual senses to find the water source. It takes time and looks more like planting, watching, and waiting. Show them how to smell the rain, feel the rain, stomp in the rain, dance in the rain, and drink in the rain. This is what discipleship looks like. Only religion passes out cups of water and a map to a dry well. Religion hides the water making it available only to an exclusive club of "church leaders." This is actually control, which is a form of witchcraft. If you are growing weary in well doing, analyze the situation you are in and consider your motives and the motives of the ones directing and leading in the place you serve. If you discover you have gone off course, simply repent and reset your compass.

The kingdom is like a charity that chooses to do more than feed the hungry. They bring farm animals and agriculture into poverty-stricken areas because they know if they train the people how to collect eggs, milk cows, and grow their own gardens, they can survive on their own because they have access to the sources that will sustain them. We need to lead people who are thirsty to the source of life to sustain and maintain themselves.

Let's flip the page, so to speak, and explain Supernatural Love. It goes deeper than drawing from the well; it is more than doing what is expected when no one is looking. It is more than the golden rule. It's more than just being kind. It's extra, so to speak. It's like God allows you to be an extension of Himself allowing you to feel His heart and extend His love, granting you an impartation of supernatural love. He may put people in your life that He loves and allow you to feel what He feels without you having a relationship with the person first. You automatically feel compassion and love for the person the first day you meet. These types of encounters are assignments. They are people who were assigned to be in our life. To operate fully in the gifts of the spirit, we must have love for others. Without love, everything else is hindered from maturity. Love is always first.

The point is God loves people, and we have to experience His love for His people. As a precursor to the rapid growth in my faith and hunger to seek Abba, he rekindled the gift of His love for other people. It was awakened with a simple song that turned into a prayer. I discovered His Supernatural Love.

Many years ago, I switched to Christian radio broadcasting almost exclusively. I experienced a change in my thoughts and attitude by listening to praise and worship music. I have always enjoyed music. Have you felt the presence of God move in a song to compel you into a place where every word you sing connects with your spirit and forms a prayer? This has been one of the ways the Lord speaks to me. When I started to listen to Christian radio, I learned some new songs. I didn't yet realize that song lyrics can easily translate to prayers. When I sang along with the radio, although I still wasn't familiar with the ways of the Holy Spirit, I would be touched by the words I was singing. They would circumcise my heart and translate it into a prayer.

There was a popular song a few years ago that had the lyrics to help me love people the way God loves them (*"Proof of Your Love"* by *For King and Country*). I started praying and teaching my kids to pray, "Help me to love the way you love and let other people see you through me." God answered my prayer and started bringing people into my life, giving me a supernatural love for people with no explanation. It was the undeniable answer to my prayers. One of the songs that translated into a prayer was Lauren Daigle's *"Rescue."* I remember crying and understanding that God needed an army to be his hands and feet to march to the ends of the Earth to rescue his children. I remember telling my friend Pam I just wanted to be a part of the "Army." A couple of months later, I was in Panama City and had an intense encounter listening to the song *"Spirit Lead Me"* by Michael Ketterer. In this encounter, I now realize it was God answering my prayer from the *"Rescue"* song. He downloaded words into my spirit and asked me to enlist in His army. Crying, I said, "Yes, Lord, I accept."

 **PAUSE**

Let's look at some examples and journal notes to further explain love.

Additional Reference:

YouTube <u>The Supernatural Love of God Sara George's Love Notes from Heaven</u>:
<u>https://www.youtube.com/watch?v=n3v5dEmDx20</u>

An Example of Supernatural Love

*"And this hope will not lead to disappointment. For we know how dearly God loves us because he has given us the Holy Spirit to fill our hearts with his love." -**Romans 5:5 NLT***

"He has told us about the love for others that the Holy Spirit has given you."

–   Colossians 1:8 NLT

My first memories of experiencing supernatural love were as a young girl. I watched "Feed the Hungry" about starving children in Africa. I didn't know who the Holy Spirit was, but looking back, he was with me. I would be so concerned about the children and try to figure out how to send my coins to help. I remember crying while watching those kids. This love compelled me to sponsor a child in a third-world country as a high school student with income from my first job. I was moved by love and compassion bringing forth an action.

The Magnet Analogy

The Lord gave me an analogy that may help explain Love. He showed me it's like magnets coming together. Naturally, we are drawn together like magnets to our natural parents. In the same way, God draws us to Himself. I imagine the toddler toy where you match the shapes to drop into the bucket. There is a place inside each of us that is designed to receive our Heavenly Father. It's a God-shaped hole that can only be filled with Him. It is a space or a shape or a magnet that can only be filled by Abba. The Holy Spirit explained it to me using this magnet analogy. It's simply an analogy that helped me heal and understand relationships a bit better.

People are created with different size magnets. Some people were created with larger magnets than others. I believe that the people who often struggle with rejection are the same ones given the assignment to love "BIG." The big heart is this big magnet that desires relationships and belonging perhaps more than others, and the enemy uses this against us when we don't understand why we are feeling rejected.

The big-hearted person thinks everyone feels this desire equally, but the truth is that not everyone has the same calling and assignment. Not everyone has a magnet the same size. The bigger your magnet, the more you need that connection. Each one is given unique gifts for their personal callings. As you grow in your relationship with Christ and surrender your relationships to him, He will fill those desires of your heart. When we realize not everyone is created the same, we can give more mercy and can fight off attacks of rejection.

Everything the enemy meant for evil, the Lord can turn around for our good and His glory. If we are experiencing a level of rejection, we can relate to the rejection Jesus Christ Himself suffered. This understanding makes us vessels to see others well. We become sensitive and discerning, which equips those who are called to minister to the forgotten and rejected.

An Example of a Codependent Friendship

One day, I was upset, feeling sorry for myself. I felt like I had been taken advantage of by a particular friend in that season of life. I now can recognize this relationship was a codependency, but at the time, I wasn't mature enough to recognize my error. As I was airing out my feelings to the Lord, he began to speak to my heart. I had worked hard to be a good friend. In my flesh, I desired friends, so I thought if I was a good friend, being the type of friend, I wanted, I would, in return, have those relationships I so desperately thought would fill the void in my life.

The plan failed. Instead, I was left feeling taken advantage of on top of feeling rejected. I had more acquaintances of convenience rather than true friendships. In my moaning and groaning to the Lord, he asked me a question. He asked me, "What was your motive for doing all of those favors?" I had to think about it, and I responded, "So I would have friends." Then he asked me, "Why do you want friends?" He said, "If your motive is anything other than leading others to Jesus and showing them my love, it's the wrong one." I was suddenly convicted. My conviction led to repentance and surrender. I told Jesus, "I'm done trying to make friends. I will let you do it instead." My friendships quickly turned around, and I have met many like-minded believers since I surrendered.

The best friendships are with people who have an intimate relationship with Jesus. Two people who have already surrendered their lives to live for Christ and are serving him side by side are the friends that become family. It's the analogy of two people who have already inserted God into the God-shaped hole, two complete people living life with a common goal to spread the gospel side by side. Instead of two people seeking to fill a missing void that will never be filled with anyone other than our Creator.

Jesus replied, "Who is my mother? Who are my brothers? Then he looked at those around him and said, "Look, these are my mother and brothers. Anyone who does God's will is my brother and sister and mother." -Mark 3:33-35. NLT

An Example of a Fruit of Love

Scripture References

Numbers 28:2, Deuteronomy 33:16, 1 Samuel 30:27,

Proverbs 19:6, 1 Corinthians 1:27-31

Additional Reference:

YouTube Random Acts of Roses Sara George's Love Notes from Heaven:
https://www.youtube.com/watch?v=u4YDdQHSl21

In the spring of 2019, I received a Word from the Lord that started as a thought and turned into a strategy or revelation I call "Random Acts of Roses." I love my community by passing out random vases of roses. I have always appreciated flowers and loved picking them. When I was little, this got me in trouble more than once. My mother had to teach me not to pick flowers in yards. She said they were meant to adorn and beautify a home. When I planted my rose garden initially, I didn't think about picking them. In the spring of 2019, I was reminded of scriptures mentioning gift giving and opening doors by bringing gifts to gatekeepers. I was also reminded of Scripture speaking about first fruit offerings. Tithing can and should be much more than financial. I believe it is intended to be time, money, and resources. Anything and everything we have been given, even a garden overflowing with roses. I had to unlearn my childhood lesson. I was quite honored to use my garden resources to bless other people.

The Creator of all things created the roses in my yard, and I offer Him the first fruits by bundling bouquets of the most beautiful spring roses and giving them away. I started with a few teachers at schools and continued to pick an abundance of blossoms almost daily and deliver them all over town. I would allow the Holy Spirit to guide me to whom he desired. It is absolutely a joy and delight to pick and arrange them and then randomly brighten someone's day with such a surprise gift.

Obedience moved love to mature into compassion. Compassion delivered hope and fulfilled God's promise of joy. I never anticipated the joy that would be found in both the giving and receiving of roses. It was a transfer of wealth, so to speak. If we have the power to do something to turnaround someone's day, why would we withhold it?

When we choose to live in intimacy with Christ soaking in all he has for us we are richly blessed to live an overflow lifestyle. Joy cannot be bought or sold, but like love it can be drawn up out of our wells to the point of overflow. Through an overflow of intimacy, the ministry assignment "Random Acts of Roses" was born. Love and joy were passed out with each rose delivering smiles, laughter, and encouragement turning around and brightening otherwise dull days. I believe love and joy are more powerful than the US Dollar.

Fall of 2019, I heard the Lord speak expansion over my garden. I started planning my landscaping and purchasing border stones twenty or so at a time. I ordered new rose bushes. I was busily planning and working in my garden as COVID-19 arrived in my home state in March 2020. Unfortunately, I could not deliver roses in May of 2020, but the shutdowns and extra time at home were perfect for garden expansion.

I found myself in a season of growth. I was reading the Bible and spiritual books, worshipping on my front porch, and soaking in the beauty of God's creation. Spring 2023 will have brought the expansion into a fully mature garden.

Roses can take three seasons to reach maturity. I believe God is speaking something special in this place of beauty, growth, and rest. In 2021, he had me declare that it was a prayer garden. He gave me a vision of preaching on the hill right in my little front yard. The anticipation and wonder of the fulfillment of serving the King of Kings in this bold way is a present waiting to be unwrapped.

I can see clearly now that the garden I planted in the physical was a prophetic act being replicated in the spiritual. A garden of young people was planted in my life in 2020. In 2023, these young people have matured into overflow. The fruit from their lives started to mature and ripen. These same students are planting their own spiritual gardens now. I watch them start their own movements leading by example of what it looks like to follow Christ by discipling others.

Let's pause and pray this short prayer.

Scripture References

Mark 3:33, 1 Corinthians 1:27-31

Lord,

Forgive me for seeking friendships with the wrong motives. Forgive me for not sitting in the rain seeking You. Forgive me for wasting time while many souls were being lost. Show me the ways I have been blessed by You. Release keys of creative, simple strategies to allow me to be an extension of Your love. Forgive me for pleasing man and not You. Take over and connect me to the ones You desire to use in my life to position me into kingdom alignments. Let my relationships honor You and serve Your kingdom instead of my own. Let me partner with you to deliver hope, joy and promises with compassion here on Earth.

In Jesus' Name,

Amen.

Chapter 4 Journal Notes

SARA C GEORGE

CHAPTER 5

THE HIGHEST FORM OF WORSHIP IS OBEDIENCE

It's time to get in the canoe and start to flow down the river as we discover how to follow God's voice, obeying his instructions.

"If you love me, obey my commandments."

- *John 14:15 NLT*

"I have loved you even as the Father has loved me. Remain in my love. When you obey my commandments, you remain in my love, just as I obey my Father's commandments and remain in his love. I have told you these things so that you will be filled with my joy. Yes, your joy will overflow! This is my commandment: Love each other in the same way I have loved you. There is no greater love than to lay down one's life for one's friends. You are my friends if you do what I command. I no longer call you slaves because a master doesn't confide in his slaves. Now you are my friends since I have told you everything the Father told me. You didn't choose me; I chose you. I appointed you to go and produce lasting fruit so that the Father will give you whatever you ask for, using my name. This is my commandment: Love each other." – **John 15:9-17 NLT**

"Jesus replied, 'All who love me will do what I say. My Father will love them, and we will come and make our home with each of them. Anyone who doesn't love me will not obey me. And remember, my words are not my own. What I am telling you is from the Father who sent me.'" – **John 14:23-24 NLT**

It's time to get in the canoe and start to flow down the river as we discover how to follow God's voice, obeying His instructions. In God's eyes, obedience measures our love for Him. It's a natural flow to move from talking about love to talking about obedience. Obedience is simple: just do it. Do what is asked to your best ability and do it without delay. This doesn't require teaching instead encouragement that builds faith through understanding and examples.

When the Holy Spirit speaks and leads you into a task, it will be something that you don't want to do initially. The fact that it isn't something that you want to do or say allows you to start to recognize the voice of the Holy Spirit speaking to you. You will learn to recognize His voice because the assignments line up with His character and nature. As His beloved sheep, we know His voice and it resonates in our spirits by the knowledge revealed as He clearly portrays Himself in the Holy Bible. He has many names and revelations about His character in the Bible. You will know the voice and ideas are not your own. A good place to start if you are uncertain of a voice, is to open the Bible and start reading and studying it for yourself. When you step up to the plate and obey the Holy Spirit, each step of obedience will bring you more faith. Remember, we are citizens of Heaven and not Earth. We should live like we are in the heavenly realm. I encourage you to DIVE into obedience. Remember, it doesn't matter what people think. It only matters that you heard His voice and jumped into the metaphorical ocean in response to Him.

PAUSE

During this training season of 2020, the Lord gave me a wonderful spiritual father whom I affectionately call Coach, Pastor Rick Mendoza. He watches over my growth, and encourages me to continue moving forward. He intercedes for me, listens to all my videos, and reads my prophetic words and dreams. This relationship has been a safe place for me to ask questions and grow in the things of God. Often, we don't understand what God is doing, but God knew I needed Pastor Rick in my life. Sometimes, I wanted to know why other leaders or people I looked up to didn't offer help, reach out, or disciple me. I can now see clearly that it wasn't assigned to anyone except Coach Rick. God handpicked and ordained this man to specifically be my spiritual father. I didn't have to go out looking for a Coach; instead, God gave him to me in a divine encounter on a beachfront balcony. I want to let you know when it's God's plan, His ways are not forced and pushed. Instead, they are natural encounters that flow into kingdom relationships without seeking or striving.

UNPAUSE

I think it's relevant now to tell you about the lighthouse. I had never visited a lighthouse. March 2020 I was on vacation and there was a lighthouse in a nearby town. I felt compelled to take a drive and check it out. All throughout vacation I noticed signs with pictures of lighthouses or the word lighthouse. One was Lighthouse Church. Toward the end of the trip, I looked back through the pictures we had taken and noticed that many of them had light beams like beacons of light shining down on us. I soon realized that God was revealing his word through the lighthouse, much like the parable of the house built upon the rock.

We toured the lighthouse, took pictures and had a picnic in the park. I was seeking clues for a video message coming up, and I did some research on lighthouses. Some interesting things I discovered about lighthouses include a solid rock foundation, not sinking sand. The solid rock we stand on is faith in Jesus Christ. A lighthouse is marked with a high-water mark and a low-water mark. In modern generations, we have been in low water for a long time, but it's getting ready to rain. It will be a cleansing rain. The water will get higher, and the wind will begin to blow, creating waves of revival, but it will also stir up and cause turbulence in the water. A lighthouse is a guide for sinking, swirling lost sailors. We can choose to increase our light and become like the lighthouse, guiding people into the glorious light of the Savior. We won't miss the storm. Instead, we will STAND through the storm, planted on a rock of faith in Jesus Christ. We are called to unite in prayer, seeking the Father's voice to stand and weather the storm. It's time for war. Call out the warriors. When you fear the Lord, you don't have to be afraid of the storm. Instead, rise up and stand on the rock with your eyes looking for Jesus. Just like a dancer or gymnast picks out a point to steady themselves, called "spotting," we spot looking at Jesus so that when the turbulent waters come, we remain focused on his face. If you get turned around or dizzy for a moment, it's ok. Refocus on the light.

An act of obedience opened the door for the new thing God was about to do in my life. As I have grown to discern the voice of God and willfully follow His instructions, He asked me if I would really go wherever He leads. My family attended a worship and prophetic meeting with Daniel Pontious in August 2020. The prophet asked who wanted more of God. I don't know how many people responded, but I believe it was a high percentage of those there, including my daughter and myself. Daniel ministered, prayed, and spoke over many who came forward. Towards the end of the night, after most had left, my daughter was overwhelmed with a vision of a young teen girl standing on a pier, ready to jump. It was the assignment given to her by her asking for more of God. My daughter felt an urgency to rescue this girl. She could see her and knew what she looked like and where the pier was located. It was in Panama City Beach, Florida. Confirmation from my friend Susan led me to accept the rescue assignment. My daughter of thirteen had to have me be willing to listen and respond to her at that moment. I said, "Yes, I believe you, and we will go." It was approximately midnight on Friday night, and we left by noon on Saturday for an eleven-hour drive to rescue the one.

I contacted my local friends from Panama City about the assignment and they joined us in prayer. My beautiful friend Joy, who was at the time more of an acquaintance than a friend, invited us into her home for this spontaneous trip since we did not have any reservations. This is an example of how the Kingdom of Heaven operates and provides for our every need through the obedience of other believers. We are called to respond as His hands and feet. Joy has had opportunities to house ministers in her home over the years and has a special gift of hospitality. She made us feel like family. Joy, John, Frannie, and several others prayed with us about the assignment. We were given even more insight and revelation about the girl. We felt we knew what type of clothes she would be wearing; we had a possible name; we knew her situation involved some sexual abuse. We spent almost a week in Panama City. We were prepared to be prompted by the Holy Spirit to go to the pier at any random moment. I believed we would be woken up at a random hour of the night because a middle-of-the-day crowded pier didn't seem like an obvious choice for an attempted jump. We listened, engaged, and prepared. One evening, Joy and her husband, Doug went to the county pier, and they prayed over the pier. Joy saw a young girl that could match the description of the one we were looking for. When they left the pier and got in the car, she tuned into a local live broadcast church service near the pier, and at that moment, randomly, they called out a spirit of suicide. We were actively engaged in prayer and on alert for further instructions.

On that trip, we did not meet the young girl in person. It seems it was simply an assignment of intercession and a test of obedience that would slingshot us into our next season with the Lord. We believe that one day, we will have a divine encounter that will connect the dots and allow us to meet her.

REWIND

As I type the word "Rewind," I see my friend Susan in a conversation using that term. She's like, "Whoa, hold up, let's rewind," then I have a vision of an old VCR tape from the 80s in the rewind machine, so not knowing God was using her that day, she greatly contributed to the creative style of this written work. All things are for a purpose. Thank you, Susan, for being a part of my story!

To give a little background to how prayer works and how we partner with God to be his hands and feet, I need to remind you at this point in the story that throughout late winter and spring of 2020, I had connected with the Lauren Daigle's song "Rescue" in a very intimate way and prayed to have God use me. At that moment, I didn't know my daughter had a list of prayers for the month, and on the list was "Let me rescue someone." Don't be surprised when he answers your prayers and tests your heart for obedience. It sounded like a far-fetched mission if you didn't know the background. The few people I talked to about the assignment may have thought I was a bit crazy. After all, how would I possibly find the one? God gave me a heart for the broken, and I cannot bear the thought of knowing I could make a difference and then choosing not to act.

 UNPAUSE

While on this journey, God started speaking to me about future assignments. I spent quite a lot of time on that trip praying and bonding with some fellow godly women, seeking God's face and praying over "The One." Unexpectedly, on that trip, the Holy Spirit started to put thoughts into my heart to buy furniture for my living room. I was having a conversation with Joy while we rinsed sand from our feet on the beach boardwalk. I remember the conversation just like it was yesterday. We talked about how you could rent a beach condo in the off-season for a very reasonable rate. I said, "I would really like to bring some friends down to visit." I even stopped to ask the condo managers about it because they were out at the beach that afternoon as well. When we were walking back to the pool, I said, "You know, I believe I need to buy some new furniture." We also spoke about stocking up the pantry. Several years before, my husband and I shopped and picked out a certain set of couches for our living room but didn't buy them. God was telling me to go ahead and buy them. I knew exactly what I was supposed to buy. I also knew why I was supposed to buy them. He told me people would be sleeping in my living room. These were nice reclining leather couches. I thought to myself, that was three years ago. There is no way they still have the same couch for sale. When I returned home, I went to the store and sure enough they were there. I looked at the price and decided I don't really need this furniture. It's a bit too expensive. I dismissed the idea and asked God, "Well, why can't they sleep on the old furniture? It's good enough, and I don't have to have the new ones." This was the end of August. I completely dismissed the idea; however, by the second part of September, God again told me to go buy those couches.

It was such an odd request and not without expense, so I talked to a couple of trusted spirit-filled sisters in Christ and asked them what they thought. I didn't get a firm confirmation. I wanted one, but God didn't think it was necessary. One friend thought God wouldn't ask me to go into debt for him. One thought maybe he meant he would give me a new couch. I thought, maybe I would hear someone is in real need of a couch and I would offer them my set and buy the new furniture. Nevertheless, I still felt very strongly about the instructions. I did notice I received a deposit in my account that was not earned income, and it would cover over half the cost. I mentioned it to my husband, and he wasn't against the idea. I was packing for a short trip and flying out the next day, but nevertheless, I took time to drive back to that furniture store. I got there and spoke with a nice salesman who said the furniture I was looking for was currently out of stock. I asked him to write down the specific pieces and prices for me. I returned to my car, and I sat down and said, "God, why am I here?" I went back into the store and explained to the salesman "I really don't need any furniture, but God told me to come, so I was just wondering if there is anything for which you need prayer over in your life? Perhaps I could pray for you." He kind of chuckled and said, "No, ma'am. I can't think of anything." He told me he did a lot of praying in the store himself. I wasn't there for the salesman. It was for the furniture. I got back in my car and pulled out of the parking lot, hearing the song by Dolly Parton, *Then There Was Jesus*," and I knew I was exactly where I was supposed to be. I almost called back before I got on the plane to put in my official order for those couches.

So that brings me to the song, *"Then There Was Jesus."*

Let me explain how that song became such a strong confirmation for me. A few weeks earlier, I was reading a book that pointed out that when you hear something in repetition, it is definitely God speaking, so you should begin asking Him, "What are you saying?" So, between the rescue mission and the furniture event, I was with my husband overnight, about an hour from the house, and all weekend, I kept hearing the song *"Then There Was Jesus."* I understood this repetition was not insignificant. I felt he was trying to say, "You are on the right path," or that he was with me at that moment. I understand a skeptic might just say, "Oh, that was just a popular song; it doesn't mean anything," but trust me, after you start to recognize the voice of God, it wasn't just a coincidence. As I type this, I feel like it's one of those movies that keep going backward into a memory bank. So, let me go in reverse once more.

 REWIND

Throughout the summer, starting in early spring, I wanted some new furniture for my front porch. I kept looking at different options. The only one I liked was overpriced. I didn't buy it. This particular weekend, as I was driving to meet my kids at the lake, "Then There Was Jesus" started playing, and I suddenly perked up and paid attention to my surroundings. I happened to pass by a flea market with some wooden furniture displayed outside. I made a quick call to my husband to let him know I was turning around and would catch up shortly. Here is another detail showing that that was God's plan. My husband had driven his car separately that weekend, although I didn't really understand why. We went to the same place for the weekend with friends. It didn't make any sense, but like I said, if it doesn't make logical

sense, it's God. It was Sunday, and I didn't even know if this little store was open, but they were open. I turned around and went back to check on the prices. It was beautifully hand-crafted and the cheapest furniture I had seen all summer. I purchased a single-seater porch swing. I don't think I have ever seen one before. My porch is small, and I always wanted a porch swing, but my porch was too small for the standard size. If I had not been driving my van, I wouldn't have been able to make the purchase. Another piece of information is that if my husband hadn't made plans to stay an hour from our house overnight, we would never have traveled the road that led me to the swing. Can you see there is a purpose in all things? Just trust and go with the holy flow, and don't fight or try to force things to happen. When following the Holy Spirit, it's a very organic flow.

FAST FORWARD

The evening before my flight, after the trip to the furniture store, I went to my Monday night prayer meeting, and I told my friend Brittany what I did and how I felt like I was supposed to buy these couches, and it just didn't make sense. She encouraged me by asking, "Do you want more of God?" I said YES, and she said, "Well, why are you waiting? Just Do IT." I went ahead and flew out for a trip that week, and while I was away, my friend, Jan, messaged me and said, "You know, if you were serious about having a retreat, I want to come and bring a friend."

PAUSE

This statement "Do you want more of God" God repeated this phrase through multiple people in this season of my life. It preceded some amazing encounters allowing me to grow in my faith. I pray if you hear someone ask you this question you will recall my testimony and recognize God has something he is trying to do in your life to move you onto the path he has assigned you.

"You know, if you were serious about having a retreat, I want to come and bring a friend." This random comment is an important confirmation on my journey. In the coming sections I give testimony about the retreat God assigned me February 2021. This random comment was a part of the process identifying God's plan. Sometimes the clues can be quite subtle, but when we are tuned in to the Father we can easily find them.

A month earlier, I mentioned to some girls casually, that we should have a retreat. This casual reminder made me think more seriously if a retreat was possible.

I thought it would be nice to have some friends visit me. I have a gift of hospitality and experience in event and party planning. Hospitality comes naturally to me. I love to host friends of God. I spent a few years as an event planner in my 20s. I now understand my event planning job was training for God's future assignments.

Let me tell you about my friend Jan. I met her at the beach. I will start by saying 2020 was one of the best years of my life. Now, I should testify further to explain how we ended up on the beach that day I met Jan. Spontaneously, my daughter started saying she wanted to go to Panama City Beach for a vacation. We planned for my daughter to be water baptized in the ocean and this seemed like a great opportunity. (Several years before, I had been on the beach and witnessed a youth group being baptized in the ocean, and it was just beautiful.) After the Holy Spirit baptism, the previous February, my daughter, and I started discussing water baptism. She was ready to be baptized and wanted our friend John to baptize her in the ocean and this was the first opportunity.

We usually don't go on vacation that time of year, but Covid made it possible. The kids had been home from school for several weeks, and everyone was ready for a change of scenery, so we took my daughter's whimsical advice and left the next day. You see, when you are flowing with God, you must let go and be flexible. All these details made it possible for the divine encounter God had preplanned to align naturally for me to meet Jan. This is how I roll, or shall I say flow following the prompting of the Holy Spirit. I feel like it's important to share the full process to help others start to identify Holy Spirit promptings in their own lives.

Jan is a woman after God's own heart. I met Jan by being obedient to God. I was preparing to do a live social media devotional on the beach. I knew I couldn't go live without getting in the throne room to hear what God wanted to say. I was staying in a one-room hotel and didn't want to wake up my family, so I walked across to the pool deck early one morning with my Bible, notebook, phone, and speaker. I had several confirmations that morning. Jan introduced herself while I was looking out at the ocean and belting my heart out along with my little red speaker worshipping God. After all, we should be free to worship anywhere. This was the first time I had ever done anything like that by myself and in public. It was a big step, but I wanted God's Word. Jan came over, sat beside me, and gave me a prophetic word about my life. At 43 years old, I had never received a prophetic word from anyone outside of praying with a friend or talking to someone I knew who may have said something in conversation, but I most likely didn't recognize it as a word of knowledge or a word of wisdom. This was different. It was an undeniable moment I will never forget. I told Jan why I was worshipping and invited her to watch my live post-devotional. I also invited her to attend a beach church service with me the next day. She and her friend came to church the next day, and we connected further. I introduced her and her friend Angie to my good friend John. As a part of that encounter, I became quite good friends with Angie as well and both Angie and Jan ended up continuing a friendship with my friend John.

On a side note, on the drive down, I walked into a random gas station, and there, right at the entrance, was a rack of books with a title that just stuck out like God shined a ray of light and said, "This is for you." I bought a copy of "100 Names of God" by Christopher D. Hudson and two matching journals for myself and my daughter. That book has been such an inspirational piece that has facilitated my spiritual walk. God wants us to know His character so we can trust him. After all, how do we know his *character without knowing his names and his stories? A devotional from that book was part of my inspiration that morning I encountered Jan.*

 UNPAUSE

The Retreat, The Anniversary, and The Couch

While on the anniversary trip Fall 2020, I read some amazing books and received many downloads from Holy Spirit. On the return flight, he gave me my marching orders. He said I was to have a "retreat." I asked him when, and I heard February. I asked him when it was in February. He said Valentine's weekend because he loves us and wants to be our Valentine. He also told me to start a weekly conference call on a particular book, like a book club.

I returned home and went back to the furniture store and bought the back-ordered couches. I was told they would be delivered before the end of October. I was on cloud nine for a few days and continued to ask Abba questions about the retreat. When I asked him about a theme, he said it was an engagement party. Then he told me it would be an upper room just like in Acts: a place where we wait for him. I held these thoughts in my heart.

During the fall I was immersed in seasonal work at my office. After hours, I continued studying and seeking God, holding book club conference calls and attending prayer meetings and regular church services at our local church and other regional area churches.

I found time to randomly order some decorations and party ware with a "Happy Birthday Jesus" theme. I didn't have a date or particular plan to have a party, but felt compelled to prepare for one. As the items came in, I set them aside. I ordered cupcakes and cake toppers, plates, cups, balloons, a couple of garden flags, and some little party favor crowns. I didn't know why I ordered the crowns, but somehow, they seemed to go with the theme.

My new couches were delivered before November as expected. I wasn't home when the delivery driver dropped them off.   I was excited to see how they looked and asked my daughter to send me a picture. In the corner near the couches, I could see this light beam shining down. The light represented further confirmation. It wasn't coming from a lamp or window, but straight down from the ceiling. Needless to say, we were very pleased with the new furniture.

 PAUSE

Here are a few notes from that beach trip about "The Lighthouse."

Additional Reference YouTube

Become a Lighthouse Sara George's Love Notes from Heaven:

www.youtube.com/watch?v=EOC0ikE2Wl0

The Lighthouse

A lighthouse – a person who has accepted the position and enlisted in God's army, has surrendered, and is willing to go. A lighthouse is a firmly planted, unwavering beacon of light on a solid foundation (rock). The further away you are from the lighthouse, the broader the beams stretch. The lost will be seeking the lighthouse during dark storms. Lighthouses reunite families. Lighthouses don't move, they draw the lost to the light. Lighthouses are engineered with a low water mark and a high-water mark. They are powerful light sources, more than flickering candles. They are beacons of light; light is magnified through a lens and directs lost ships. Lighthouses are prepared and ready for the storm. Rain brings storms, and with storms come wind and waves.

Prepare for the Storm

Are you in the lighthouse or on a ship? Get ready. The waves are coming. Storms, waves, and wind rock boats and can push them off course, causing them to get lost. In a storm, you can't stop the waves, but a lighthouse is the guide, leading the ships to shore with their strong beacon of light. People are in the storm, rocking and waving, thinking they are about to capsize, but the lighthouse has a high-water mark and will stand tall on a firm foundation. Let the lights unite. If the shore was marked with a clear light, the ships could find their way. The more lighthouses, the stronger the chance the ship will make it to shore. Lighthouses can only be seen in darkness. The storm comes for all of us. It isn't personal, but the rain pours everywhere. It's how you receive the rain.

Let it rain. I am standing firm with a clear light.

"Come to ME. I WILL lead you and not just you. I will lead ALL because you are not special. I come for ALL my people. Unite and STAND FIRM. Step in FAITH. The Holy Spirit will lead you in the path of righteous living."

"I will give those who ask and seek a clear light (wisdom and discernment) you will learn to fear the Lord, so I can mark and protect you healing your body."

Then, I will pour out my RAIN.

Nothing can stop the RAIN from pouring.

The storm is coming. Be Prepared! In the storm pray, seek, and look for the light. It will be a floodlight shining in the dark.

Chapter 5 Journal Notes

_____

_____

_____

_____

_____

_____

_____

_____

_____

_____

_____

_____

_____

_____

_____

_____

_____

_____

_____

_____

_____

_____

_____

_____

_____

_____

_____

_____

_____

SARA C GEORGE

CHAPTER 6

GOD IS DOING SOMETHING NEW

New Furniture, Party Favors, and a New Language

But forget all of that; it is nothing compared to what I'm going to do.

-Isaiah 43:18 NLT

Evalyn and Natalie

The next phase of the journey opened a new chapter in heaven. In late 2020, God pressed a pause button and shifted my assignment for a season. I did not record any more prophetic or teaching messages until March 20, 2021. It was exactly a three-month resting period. You might wonder what happened during that silent period. It was new and absolutely amazing. The last week in December 2020, I hosted a youth sleepover. It started with Evalyn, one of the students near my daughter's age who wanted to talk about a scripture in Revelation. I decided since it was Christmas Break, we might as well have some of the girls from church stay for a sleepover. I told my friend Coach Rick about the sleepover and we both felt there was something we needed to do to prepare. While the students were in evening youth class, I felt compelled to have personal worship time in my living room. Coach Rick simultaneously felt compelled to intercede in prayer. After my time with the Lord, I picked the girls up and we headed to my house for what we didn't yet know would be one of the best nights of our lives.

The kids were simply being kids. They played the card game Spoons. During the card game, suddenly, Evalyn was spontaneously crying and quite disturbed. I told the kids to go pray for her. They responded, and she recovered. It wasn't long after that we went for a group walk. I talked with Evalyn while we were walking about her questions. She shared that she keeps hearing the word "Fire," and we talked about how God speaks to people. Fire is a purifying element or character trait of the Holy Spirit. The Holy Spirit is often represented as water, wind, and fire.

Later, we were in the living room, and one of the girls wanted some soda. I don't stock carbonated beverages in my home, so I sent my son, and the only other teen boy present out to the store. While the boys were gone, I asked the girls if they knew what their spiritual gifts were. They seemed unsure, so I said, "Let's pray about that." I asked the students to take notes and write down anything they felt the Holy Spirit was saying.

Evalyn said, "Something's about to happen." As we started praying for the first student the kids prayed in their prayer languages as I prayed in English. I prayed for words of wisdom about her gifts and blueprints from heaven for her life. As I prayed in English, I suddenly said, "Fire, Evalyn Fire." I didn't plan to say this. I was, actually, praying for someone who was not Evalyn. It just came out. As I spoke the word, Evalyn jumped up off the floor and did a little dance in the air, kicking her legs and then "BAM," flat out on the hardwood floor she went with no one to catch her.

The Holy Spirit filled the house, and we continued praying for each teen there in the same manner. As the evening progressed, two of the girls were travailing in the spirit, interceding in prayer through cries and groaning. They were overcome with compassion for others and the desire to see people set free. Three different girls fell out under the power of God that night. Evalyn spoke with strong authority to the enemy and kicked him out of my house by yelling and slamming doors. Hadley had the joy of the Lord filling the room with laughter. I had not EVER experienced this kind of manifested presence of God before. God was pouring out NEW WINE in my living room. I am absolutely honored that the Creator of the universe descended upon MY home. What an incredible honor it was to witness the Lord move in such power. This night lit a fire within my heart, and relationships were forged in fire. It was the beginning of something new and it was the first of many meetings and encounters with the ones God chose for me to love. The teens and I pursued God passionately on my living room floor for the next few weeks. Jesus met us and built up each person's faith through healing, miracles, prayers, and friendships until I was commissioned to leave for the next assignment.

 PAUSE

New Furniture, Party Favors, and a New Language

The new couches were for the teenagers who spent many nights sleeping in my living room. The Happy Birthday Jesus theme party favors and the little crowns I ordered in the fall, God ordained for use during our Revival Nights. The Holy Spirit instructed me during each meeting, and in one of them, we celebrated Jesus' Birthday. Each student was formally presented with a piece of prophetic jewelry based on the words of the Lord from those first couple of nights of outpouring. He had me wrap them by placing them inside the miniature crowns, and He gave the Word for them to become His followers and pursue Him because He wanted to receive them into His Kingdom with crowns. It was such a beautiful word.

During this sweet, intimate time, the Lord led us into different ways to hear His voice and increased our faith. Every student witnessed firsthand miracles with their own eyes. What amazing days and nights we had together in the Glory Cloud. In that season when I entered my living room in the early mornings for prayer and my personal time with the Lord, I felt an electric tangible presence and excitement that I could not deny. It felt like what I remembered feeling at Christmas as a child. I had so much excitement it was difficult doing everyday life. The presence of God was so exciting I could hardly be still, anticipating more. I worshipped using song and dance in my living room while the world slept. Oh, how I treasure those moments as I wait for the next wave of Glory!

A little side note from my journal:

Revival is God's manifestation of Himself walking into the room. Revival brings an understanding of the fear of the Lord, leading to conviction, repentance, and redirecting. The fire of God comes to purify and transform His bride, bringing humility and a greater understanding of the power and fear of the Lord.

It was during these revival weeks that it SUDDENLY happened. The gift of unknown tongues I had prayed to receive suddenly came upon me. One day as I was driving through my neighborhood, I heard the Holy Spirit download to me and tell me that the delay I experienced in receiving my prayer language was directly related to my assignment. I understood in a moment that in an outpouring of the Holy Spirit, someone must lead, and there needed to be understanding of the prayer by others in the room. If I had already received an unknown tongue, my confidence and boldness to pray in my native tongue may have been hindered. I may not have wanted to step out and lead prayer that night. But with the practice the Lord had given me in public speaking and prayer on live videos, He gave me security in letting the Holy Spirit flow through me, using my voice to carry forth His plans. Many people are uncomfortable praying out loud and prefer to pray quietly in their prayer language in group settings. I needed to be heard and willing to lead with understanding. I just started to get a few syllables of "babble." I wondered if perhaps I was receiving the gift of tongues. I had heard other people describe something like this happening to them. A day or two later, in corporate worship at church, as I worshipped the Lord, the new language just started pouring out.

 UNPAUSE

It was February 2021, and the assignment from heaven sent me to Panama City Beach, Florida. I received the assignment in October 2020 to go to the beach. I trusted the Lord every step of the way. I didn't want to leave the revival in my living room, but I trusted that God had a plan set in advance, and I knew without any hesitation that it was time to move into the next season. So, I left my home and living room revival for a temporary home in an upper room beach condo. I had a women's retreat one weekend, and before I left for Florida, one of the moms, my friend Heather, agreed to bring our living room revival to the beach. On the days between the women's and youth retreat, I had family and friends coming to stay. I didn't realize that the entire month, God was planning a retreat. The guests just flipped in and out, and they didn't all know they were there to meet Jesus. Nevertheless, he met each one.

 **PAUSE**

Heather has been the best support and the most encouraging mom I could ask to join me on these adventures I have been called to fulfill. Without her driving students and being my co-mom, so many of these adventures would not have been possible.

▶ **UNPAUSE**

When I transitioned to the beach upper room condo for the retreats, I invited my friends Joy and Frannie to help me prepare the atmosphere. The three of us joined together. Three of us didn't seem to be a mistake. God often uses three. Three strands make a cord! We anointed and prayed over the condo. They helped me stock the pantry with tea and snacks. We tuned into a "Let Us Worship" rally and worshipped there in the upper room condo, while preparing and surrendering to whatever the Lord had planned. Joy had a vision of an angel stationed at the front door with what looked like a honey pot. She wasn't certain, but we felt the honey was for healing. We were excited to see what the Holy Spirit had in store.

God encountered us every day. We started each day with a prayer and asked the Lord to direct our steps. The day was his to interrupt as he desired. We had no schedule or agenda and only a very loose idea about what we might do each day. One morning, we started with coffee at John's Surf Shop. We spontaneously had opportunities to pray and prophesy over each other, as well as patrons, and employees. Suddenly, my friend Kim had a thought, and the Lord sent us down the road to worship, pray, and prophesy at a transitional home. The manager was there on site. She gave us a tour and gave permission for us to minister. A couple of the ladies were moved with compassion to go back and volunteer to do some cleaning in one of the shower halls. We worshipped in public spaces like Pier Park, (in front of the movie theater by the big beach ball), the beach, and out in the courtyard of a local restaurant. Each day was special and moving. We made space and room each evening to get together and just see what God had planned. We shared testimonies, giving honor and remembrance to the Lord and creating bonds.

John invited our group to lead a gathering at the Surf Shop. We all shared the role of selecting worship songs. Several of us prepared and we washed the feet of everyone who attended. Shelly gave a message, and I let the Lord use me to lead an encounter by reading "The Journey," which is included in the tools section of this book. The next day Kim got an invitation for us to come and lead a ministry service at the transitional home. I gave a short message, and we invited the attendees to let us wash their feet and pray with them.

 PAUSE

Let me explain why we chose to wash the feet of strangers. In John Chapter 13, Jesus washed the feet of his disciples.

So if I, your Lord and Teacher, have washed your feet, you also should wash one another's feet. I have set you an example so that you should do as I have done for you. Truly, truly, I tell you, no servant is greater than his master, nor is a messenger greater than the one who sent him. If you know these things, you will be blessed if you do them. - John 13:14-17 NLT

I suddenly felt new revelation and conviction to wash people's feet as Christ did. Most people take this instruction in this scripture as a metaphor, but I feel it is also a prophetic act and literal command that is overlooked. Physical acts are often considered prophetic acts of faith, understanding that we are partnering with God by faith of obedience and submission. Often, we can partner with God in what seems to make no earthly sense because God chooses to use simple things to confound the wise. This act of foot washing *is glossed over since it's no longer a custom in our culture. It seems to be interpreted as optional instead of a direct command. Let's face it; no one really wants to wash someone else's feet. There is deep revelation to be found in this passage, but in my opinion, I feel the literal interpretation is equally important.*

The Holy Spirit revealed to me that washing your feet daily is necessary because our soul gets dirty daily. Daily, we walk through life, and our soul gets dirty by exposure to the fallen world all around us. Daily we have thoughts and behaviors that if left unchecked start to influence our lives. We should intentionally wash these away daily. Dirt needs to be addressed daily. Unintentional sin tries to creep into our lives daily, and we don't need to get used to the dirt. It shouldn't look normal. We are called to be set apart from the world. Repent and turn to Christ daily. The comment by Jesus to Peter about not needing a full bath every day symbolizes not needing to daily pray the "sinners' prayer." We don't need to pray as sinners pray for salvation daily, but as children of the King of Kings, we should grow into the Fear of the Lord understanding our identity and showing honor by washing our feet before walking into the throne room. Jesus will meet you right where you are and run down the dirt road to greet you; however, there are those moments we prepare ourselves. On this journey let's be intentional to stop and reflect daily repenting and coming to God with a contrite heart. Check your posture and motives regularly with the Lord. Be cleansed in the washing of the Word. We cleanse daily through repentance and mediating on scripture. Pray and ask the Holy Spirit to bring fresh understanding as you read the Bible. This gives permission for the Word to wash you.

 UNPAUSE

A week or so after the women's retreat my friend Heather brought our living room revival students to the beach for a youth retreat weekend. We had a loose schedule and strategy to allow the students time to bond at the beach as well as engage in deep encounters with Jesus.

When they arrived on a Friday afternoon, we loaded up for the State Park Beach, where they could enjoy the beach, and have a sunset devotional on the jetties. It was beautiful. I had a couple of local friends, Alexa and Chase to give a word and share testimonies.

The next day, we had sunrise prayer at John's Surf Shop. John invited and commissioned us to help him anoint and pray over the shop and courtyard while we were there. Before we left, we lingered there to be still before the Lord with prayer and worship, "soaking" with the Holy Spirit. When you take that extra time to be in a quiet place with God, it is easier to understand him. In the lingering, a couple of the students were able to hear the Lord's response to them through visual encounters.

 PAUSE

Soaking is a slang term for being still before the Lord. It's a reference to relaxing in the bathtub. Soaking is sitting or standing with a heart postured in worship before God. Just to be in a quiet headspace letting yourself relax while listening to see if any thoughts, words, visions, or ideas come to your mind from the Lord.

 UNPAUSE

We went to visit Ms. Glenna, who was in her 80s but still ready and waiting to give her testimony and teach. She ministered to each one of us, and we worshipped and soaked with the Lord together. Saturday evening, we had a photo shoot and a beachside bonfire devotional. I asked my friend Lucas to lead the devotional since he had just released his first book "Holy Ghost and Fire," which seemed to go with the bonfire theme.

Sunday, we went to a special church service. We followed church with an afternoon on the beach. The Holy Spirit had his way in every part. It was a beautiful blend of refreshing our body and spirit. We had beautiful moments of spontaneous worship, singing in the spirit, interpretation of tongues, and many more moments of flowing in the Holy Ghost. One of my favorite encounters was a spontaneous prayer and song session. My friend, Alexa, stopped in. Prayer led to spirit-filled worship in tongues. Alexa and Evalyn echoed back and forth, a beautiful song in their spirit language. It was a picture-perfect winter beach youth weekend aesthetic in every way. My month in Florida was just the beginning of a year of being led around the country, walking in the spirit of God. It was truly a season where Mark 3:33-35 came alive with doing the work of ministry in unity partnering with the Holy Spirit. Lives were changed, hearts made new, and friendships turned into family.

I connected with a couple of women in Florida who were from Georgia. One of them, Shelly, is a pastor at a church in McCaysville, Georgia. After I returned home, I reached out and asked Shelly to let me know when they had a special event coming up, and we would visit. It wasn't a day or so later Shelly called, telling me she had scheduled a night with Eddie James and his crew to lead a worship night in just a couple of weeks.

 PAUSE

A notable detail to bring back up is, while in Florida, during the sunrise prayer with the youth, John was playing some Eddie James worship music that ministered to the students. While I was in Florida that month, I kept hearing the name Eddie James. Joy, Frannie, and John all mentioned his music and how it ministered to them. Prior to my month in Florida, I wasn't familiar with his name, music, or ministry.

 UNPAUSE

Eddie's team had called Shelly to fill a gap in their touring schedule. It was scheduled for the same week as my daughter's spring break. My daughter and I, as well as a couple of close friends Paige, Brittany, Susan, Ella, and her brothers, loaded up to take our first trip to McCaysville, Georgia.

We parked and walked into this little church in the pouring rain just in time for the event. The rain unfortunately kept many of the locals at home that night, but it was a blessing to engage and discover such a beautiful authentic group. We had the freedom to move and worship freely in the room. I heard firsthand testimony of how the blueprints of Eddie's ministry allowed him to take in the ones who were troubled, addicted, and lost bringing them into a discipleship program that transformed many of their lives. This type of ministry reminded me of Jesus and his disciples. It also made me think about the love the Lord gave me for my students and Generation Z. We were honored to share meals and conversations with Eddie and his team. Shelly gave me the honor of preparing and serving breakfast for them before they left Georgia the next morning.

After Eddie's team headed out, we were invited to discover the rich history of the area as our friends took us on a tour of the region and told us their stories. Memorials and plaques marked the land. They documented a historical   revival from the late 1800s. I looked around at each one with honor and understood that these stones were put in place to be an altar to the Lord: a place of remembrance.

 **PAUSE**

This brings me to the story of how I met my Georgia ministry friends. I met Shelly because she had connected and visited with a mutual friend, John, from the Surf Shop. My friend John mentioned her book one morning. Someone I know shared a post Shelly made on Facebook where she and some friends were making an altar and dedicating land to the Lord. On a brick, I saw the words "New Era," which was the title of the book from the weekly book call assignment the Lord had given me in October 2020. This book by Lana Vawser talks about altars. I knew at that moment I wanted to reach out to Shelly and invite her to attend the retreat in February. Can you see how God works out every tiny detail? It's mesmerizing to think of how intricate every

detail went into orchestrating this connection. How beautiful it was to see the "altars" of the Lord in that region of the country.

When I was in Georgia, Shelly introduced me to several of her local ministry friends, one of them was Lynda. Lynda and I made plans to meet at a women's conference the following month in Cleveland, TN. I was introduced to Karen Wheaton's women's ministry March 2020 when my friend John from the Surf Shop first sent me one of Karen's online messages. I discovered Karen was having a women's conference and I wanted to go. Then when Shelly introduced me to Lynda, I discovered she really wanted to go as well so it worked it out to go with Lynda. This would be my first time attending a Ramp conference, but certainly not my last. Little did I know I would make three trips to The Ramp in 2021. Karen Wheaton is the founder of The Ramp as well as a women's ministry called "Front Porch Friends."

Karen gave her testimony during the conference; she talked about how The Ramp started with just a few students praying in a shopping mall. This ministered to me greatly because I could see something similar in what the Lord was doing in my life with a handful of students. It encouraged me that this could become something much bigger than I could ask, think, or imagine. I felt assigned to bring my group of students to the Youth Conference that summer. While I was still in Cleveland at the Front Porch Friends Ramp conference, I started making hotel arrangements to bring my students to Hamilton, Alabama. Lynda and I enjoyed the conference immensely. It was beautiful, electric, and *engaging. While I was in Cleveland, the Lord woke me up with a word to write down. Let's look at it together:*

Think Upon Those Things that are Holy, Natural, and Good

IT IS FINISHED!

Meditate on the words of the Lord.

It is Written that Those who are Holy, Righteous, and Pure

Shall Inherit the Riches of the Earth and All who Dwell in It.

For the Glory of the Lord is at Hand.

I will be Your Strength and Shield and Hold You up by Your Right Hand.

High and Lifted Up, Shining by the Light of MY Glory

You will Sing Holy Holy Holy.

You Shall be My Dwelling Place.

 UNPAUSE

During the spring, after the living room revival and following the time, I was in Florida; I began seeking out opportunities to attend all kinds of Jesus events and meetings. I always invited my students to go with me. We chased Jesus all over the state. One of my favorite services was Eric Gilmour. The best way to describe the ministry and sound the Holy Spirit makes through Eric Gilmour is HONEY! His ministry flows in the revelation of intimacy and love of God. My friend Susan hosted several prophetic meetings with her friend Daniel Pontius and we attended them all.

Following the Ramp Women's conference, I got the students together to tell them about upcoming events I planned to attend, including the conference at the Ramp in Hamilton. At first, the group wasn't as excited as I was about the opportunity, but I knew it was God's plan and he would work everything out. The week after I returned from the Women's Ramp conference, we attended our first "Let Us Worship" rally held at a Little Rock park right under a bridge. Eddie James led worship alongside Sean Feucht. I had a group of my students, and their families come out to support the event. The worship was powerful and two of our student Portia and Destiney, who were a little more unsure of the Holy Spirit during the living room revival, lit up that night under the bridge at the rally while singing and dancing with Eddie James Ministry. It felt as if the spirit of God was hovering over us, beautifully blanketing the park.

If anyone in our group wasn't familiar with Eddie James before the event, after the event, we were some of his biggest fans. I must point out, though it's always important to remember the person is simply a vessel of conduit – it's Christ living in his heart and bringing out a song and energy that shines. You can tell that Eddie is a dwelling place for the joy of the Lord. The Glory of the Lord was released that day through the obedience of Sean and Eddie's ministry together. I didn't keep count of how many times the students and I were privileged to listen and worship alongside Eddie James Ministry in 2021 and into 2022. Every time Eddie came to a city near our hometown, we loaded up and went to wherever he was ministering.

As it got closer to June, suddenly overnight, families started to commit to going to the Youth Ramp Conference. Initially, the response wasn't what I had expected, but I had previously made reservations, believing it was God's plan for our group to attend. God opened the doors one by one. Chandler, one of my bonus kids, was literally permitted in the last hour before the last car left to attend the conference. God came through and increased my faith and the faith of all the students who had been praying for him to receive permission to attend.

The Youth Summer Ramp met and exceeded my anticipation. As we arrived and picked up the itinerary, we bumped right into Eddie James' young people setting up t-shirt tables. Eddie was at The Ramp, too! To attempt to put the pouring out of God at The Ramp into words is like trying to hold water in your hands. I can testify about what we saw and experienced, but it's like trying to capture the essence of a sunset on a camera. Each person could give a detailed testimony of their personal experience, but as a whole group, I can say it was a room of revelation, worship, and encounter like no other. It was as if the revival in my living room was magnified one thousand times over.

The room was full of people, and when the first note was played, the audience began to respond to the presence of God. People were trembling and on their knees in tears. It was authentic and organic worship. In our group, God honored several of our students to be vessels of prayer. They went out with boldness and fire, praying over others in the room. Boldness and courage were imparted, and they felt the voice of God inside them as it was released, transforming lives and building their individual faith. They witnessed healing and deliverance with God speaking through them. Others in our group saw visions and felt the love of his presence.

As a part of the conference, The Ramp did a creek baptism Saturday afternoon and encouraged and preached on the revelation of dying to one's old self and leaving it all behind in the water. We walked out on a dirt road towards the creek. The atmosphere was exhilarating, with a unique reverential focus and silence. It was one united focus on Jesus. There was a shift as I walked down the road and experienced walking into what I would describe as a glory cloud. Groups gathered on the sides of the creek, getting as close as they could, watching and waiting for their turn in the water. The Spirit of the Lord moved and ministered over that crowd in such a way that even those who didn't intend to get baptized were moved to experience what God was doing in the water. Memories were so special and private within each person.

The final wrap-up evening service after the baptism was a night where the Lord would have his way. Any darkness trying to hinder or hold a person captive was exposed when they accepted God's word on their forehead. "HOLY" was the word written. It was a prophetic act that shifted the room. Many fell to the floor and received prayer that night that transformed their lives. Freedom filled the room, and many stood back up a new creation in Christ Jesus, thanking and glorifying him for their freedom. I will never forget those moments and faces. I was so incredibly honored God chose me to witness and partner with him in this kingdom moment.

FAST FORWARD

In September, I went back to the Ramp with some friends, Heather, Brittany, Rhonda, Joy, Frannie, and Donna. We went to the Women's Homecoming Event for the Front Porch Friends and there I met lovely Lisa, which brings me to another dynamic encounter with the living God. We were both attending the same conference, a Karen Wheaton Homecoming Event at The Ramp in Hamilton, Alabama and were staying in the same hotel. The hotel where we stayed was one of the only ones in town, and it was full of women who loved the Lord. After the conference was over the next morning, as everyone was packing and preparing to head home, I noticed a group praying in the parking lot and decided to join them. The way I feel about God, is if he is present, I want to be there. I joined the group praying and the Lord used me to give Lisa confirmation and a word from the Lord she had been waiting to receive all weekend. Later, I found her studying on the steps and felt compelled to continue to share with her. She needed an encounter to release joy in her life. I felt that I was supposed to give her my T-shirt. It was a shirt that simply said, "JOY." I bought it at one of Eddie James' worship nights. I realized I was wearing a sweatshirt over the T-shirt at the moment that said the word "ENCOUNTER," and I knew exactly what the Lord was confirming. Lisa needed the encounter to bring her Joy.

It's such an honor to be used as a vessel for the Lord. During this season, I kept hearing, "Joy is my strength" and I remember I kept feeling compelled to get hugs from my friend Joy. A few days later, after I was home, Lisa sent me a beautiful word in a song. She sent me Lauren Daigle's "*Rescue Song*" and explained that was how she felt that day. She needed to be rescued.

PAUSE

Do you remember the encounter I had with the same song months earlier? Around the spring of 2019, I asked God to send me to be a part of his army to go out and find his lost sheep.

UNPAUSE

My heart absolutely melted at that moment, and I know we will remain a part of each other's testimony for the rest of our lives. The encounter we had was in response to a specific prayer. God is so faithful and good to hear our prayers and respond in creative ways.

FAST FORWARD

Early in 2021, I felt compelled to sign up for an online course with Lana Vawser's ministry called Positioned in Purity. The class was a blessing, in the class; I was blessed to make acquaintance with a bold woman named Aja. Aja invited me to join a prayer group called Abided Ones. This group is an international group of prophetic women that Aja disciples to grow and prosper through intercession over one another. We developed relationships that became family connections. She taught us how to rally behind one another and achieve the breakthroughs so desperately needed. It was a safe place to share and develop gifts, encouraging each other as we went. Aja's example as a prophetic voice pulled me deeper and higher as she rallied around me. She devoted her time, her heart, and her finances, proving she believed every word was from heaven's throne room. The Lord gave me a word in this season to separate the pure prophetic voice from a prophet with a false heart motive and then it was so clear to see that my dear friend Aja operates as a pure heart.

 **PAUSE**

Let's look at some journal notes the Lord gave me to help with discernment.

Additional Reference:

YouTube [Put Your Money Where Your Mouth Is Sara George's Love Notes from Heaven](https://www.youtube.com/watch?v=WK85t_exOjU): https://www.youtube.com/watch?v=WK85t_exOjU

Put Your Money Where Your Mouth Is

Where are the ones who will finance my Kingdom? Many love me in words only without action. Faith requires ACTION. Activation of faith through obedient acts will carve space inside of you to receive more faith from heaven.

Many want to be used to give a word of knowledge or prophecy, but few prove they believe the words I say because they are unwilling to step into the words. Who is willing to disciple my people? Who will follow the words with acts of obedience, sacrificing oneself by following my words with time, love, and money?

It's easy to open your mouth to release a message, but how many add faith by financially backing my Kingdom with an investment? If you take care of my people, I will take care of yours.

 UNPAUSE

As I search the father's heart for what he desires to share in this book, I'm waiting for how and where to end these stories and testimonies. You see, when you follow the Lord, it doesn't stop with one encounter or one retreat or event. It's a lifetime of transforming encounters and testimony that doesn't cease until your last breath on earth. I'm going to leave you with one last testimony to tie together the gap period of unwritten stories from 2022 and the present. It's been an incredible year, and there are so many stories I could share, but I will save them for a possible second book if it is the Lord's will.

 FAST FORWARD

Spring of 2022, I spent the month of March in Florida. During my time in Florida, I received numerous prophetic words, including a powerful Word from an Apostolic leader of Vision Church at Christian International in Santa Rosa Beach, Florida, Pastor Jane Hamon. I wasn't at church that day looking for a prophetic word, but nevertheless, during the middle of her sermon she randomly spoke directly to me prophesying about my life. This word is a powerful and significant clue in the testimony I'm sharing. She said God was connecting me with new alignments, with apostolic prophetic companies with those who are marching on assignment, I will fall in rank and march alongside them, and I will preach, teach, and prophesy. This word was given to me on Wednesday night, March 15, 2023. On March 26th, I drove home from the beach about five days earlier than originally planned, but it just felt like I was supposed to drive my daughter back home for school. While I was driving home, my friend Heather sent me a video with Eddie James talking about his health journey and relocating to Arkansas. I got home and listened to the message on Sunday night. On Monday, I spent the day unpacking and cleaning from being out of town for three weeks, and by Monday evening, I was on the phone with Eddie James, who was asking me if the youth I work with would be interested in coming alongside him as his intern dance team. The first practice was on Thursday, March 30th and the first time we danced alongside Eddie's team was on Friday, April 7th. Just like that, the words Pastor Jane Hamon spoke over my life started to manifest in the natural.

I spent 2023 partnering with Eddie James Ministries. His team worked with us and expanded my small group of students into the Eddie James Shift Internship Program. I was honored to have my first invitation to speak on a platform at a Shift Revival Night. I preached, taught, and prophesied on that stage which may seem like something small to many, but to me it was prophesy and promises fulfilled.

What an incredible year 2023 has been. Remember I wrote about the garden expansion in 2020 during COVID-19 and how it takes about three years for roses to mature? It would be spring 2023 for the expansion to reach full bloom! This garden expansion was both a physical one and prophetic one. I have a spiritual garden of students in full bloom. This is why physical acts of obedience are so important even when they don't make sense. Spring 2023 my garden of young people transformed into Shift Interns. I hope you can see the way the Lord led my story. It was a series of simple acts of obedience day by day that brought me to where I am today.

Looking for Tiffany is a boot camp of spiritual exercises to train yourself to hear the voice of God by learning the ways he communicates. In the beginning, it seems like a driving force or a hunger that propels you to search, seek, and practice. As I looked for Tiffany daily, I became hungry for more of God. I answered the call to BECOME. It's like eating a chip and then the whole bag. A hunger that cannot be satisfied teaches you the way to the narrow path. It's like a treasure map to lead you to the eye of a needle and out again on the other side of the veil into the supernatural heavenly realm of Glory!

On my journey, I have been transformed and no longer look, react, or speak like the person I once was. My hunger drove me to seek Jesus in all things and consumed my thoughts and time. There is no time to waste or lose, only time to worship, love, listen, and obey.

We must quickly carry out the tasks assigned to us by the one that sent us. The night is coming, and then no one can work - **John 9:4 NLT**

When someone is dehydrated usually, they don't know they are thirsty until they start to increase their fluids. The more they allow themselves to sip, the more they become thirsty, and their bodies start to crave more. It is the same concept spiritually. I started to drink the presence of God, and I became thirsty, craving more and more of his presence.

In this process, I began to understand what it means to "abide." Being a mature son or daughter means learning the art of abiding.

"Yes, I am the vine; you are the branches. Those who remain in me, and I in them, will produce much fruit. For apart from me you can do nothing."

- John 15:5 NLT

A simple image I think about is being grafted into Christ through his pierced side. I see this image of my feet stuck into Jesus's side and my whole body extended out diagonally just like a tree branch. It is the creative art of learning and growing in him. We train so we never have to leave his presence. To abide is to be in his presence. It's a heart posture and desire that leads us to practice abiding in him and his words and ways. In the beginning, we learn how to let him lead us. It takes practice to learn His rhythm and pace. He understands in practicing, sometimes we run too far ahead or lag too far behind, but in practice, you will find the sweet spot, and when you move too far in any direction, you will stop and return quicker.

Another visual tool that might help someone understand what it means to "Abide" is found in Psalm 23. Imagine yourself as a lamb and the Lord as a real shepherd. You would want to stay close to him for protection, to hear and be comforted by his voice and sounds so you can be led. Ideally, you want to remain in his shadow. You will mature to the place of maybe only going a few steps out of his shadow before you discern and draw back closer to him.

A more modern-day example we may be able to relate to in our culture is the bond between a dog and its master. The master and the dog share a deep bond of love. God is our Master, and we are servants of the King. He loves us unconditionally, just like we love our dogs. We don't have to do anything to receive his love. The dog loves his master so much he wants to be in his presence. The dog learns there are benefits to being near his master. He understands there is safety and comfort in his presence. His voice becomes soothing. Dogs learn their master's voice and his movements. Although they are different species, it seems the dog starts learning the human language. They start to pick out certain words and phrases, and they learn how to communicate their needs and feelings. Dogs learn their master's ways and routines. Think about training a new dog to walk on a leash. At first, it is quite a challenge, but in practice, they learn your pace and pay attention. If you start to jog, they jog too. If you slow down, they slow down. They learn to sync up to your rhythm and pace.

Practicing the presence is all about the rhythm and syncing up with Heaven. You see, the journey is not to find Tiffany, but to become the place where the presence has permission to dwell. The journey is to learn how to receive the love of the Father, so we trust him and desire to stay in His shadow. Once we get to know each other and understand how much he loves us, it becomes easier to dwell in his presence. Just like our dogs want to sleep with us or follow us from room to room constantly, just being near us, that's the same love a maturing son or daughter has for Abba. Our dogs don't have to earn our love. They simply "abide" in our presence and learn to listen to the master, obeying His commands because he loves Him.

Abba wants to be sought after. He wants to know we want Him and not just for Heaven but for Him. He created us to be His family, to love and to be loved by Him. To know and love Him is His invitation. The fear of going to Hell was never the Holy Spirit's idea. Our Father isn't a bully and has never used fear tactics to draw His children. He doesn't want just to be the obvious choice. He wants to be our everything.

My journey began with looking for how to get to the presence while God was waiting for me to go looking for Him.

Because of Christ and our faith in Him, we can now come boldly and confidently into God's presence. -**Ephesians 3:12 NLT**

We cannot live only on one sip. We must continue to drink from the living fountain. Abiding is a level of surrendering to the Holy Spirit and letting go of oneself and the desires of our flesh. It's the moment when He becomes a revelation instead of words on a page. It becomes the very source of life. The Word becomes a living, breathing well for us to drink and drink again. It's the restoration of Eden. Just like we mark our pets with collars, tags, and chips, we are MARKED by God FOREVER because we belong to Him.

And they will see his face, and his name will be written on their foreheads. -**Revelation 22:4 NLT**

I had no idea what God had planned for me when this book began to come to life summer of 2020 when my son confirmed several prophetic words as he wandered through the living room and said, "Mom, you should write a book."

Now, as I sit here typing, ready to turn this book over for publishing, I'm completely amazed and in awe of this path I'm walking on. I feel so blessed and honored that the Lord could use me to expand his kingdom. I want you to be encouraged to follow the Holy Spirit with quick obedience because the world needs who you were created to become. Time is short on this side of heaven, and all of creation is waiting for you to take your position. Don't delay one more day. Many are lost and dying every single day, and God's rescue plan is YOU; it's all of US together, uniting in one accord and marching through the Earth.

Will you join me in this exciting journey of going deeper into the heart of our creator? He's calling you to go on your own journey and to tell your own testimonies. Simply listen. He speaks in every moment. He's in the sounds of nature. He's in every vibration and sound wave. He's the source of light, the fireball providing heat and life in the sun. It all comes from his piercing glory shining down from the heavens.

And there will be no night there – no need for lamps or sun – for the Lord
God will shine on them. And they will reign forever and ever.

-Revelation 22:5 NLT

Call upon His name and surrender to Him, and the seed that has been planted within you will begin to grow. Now, it's time to write your story. What will your altar look like? How will you remember and dedicate the miracles of God on your journey?

But you are not like that, for you are a chosen people. You are royal priests, a
holy nation, God's very own possession. As a result, you can show others the
goodness of God, for he called you out of the darkness into his wonderful light.

-1 Peter 2:9 NLT

Now is the Time, Go Look for Tiffany.

Chapter 6 Journal Notes

SECTION 2

Let's start walking the winding path into the garden, a place where we grow, blossom, and flourish. Use these tools to practice and grow.

The time is coming when Jacob's descendants will take root. Israel will bud, blossom, and fill the whole earth with fruit. **- Isaiah 27:6 NLT**

TOOLS FOR YOUR JOURNEY

I am the true grapevine, and my Father is the gardener. He cuts off every branch of mine that doesn't produce fruit, and he prunes the branches that do bear fruit so they will produce even more.

-John 15:1 NLT

This next portion of the book is a series of tools, prayers, and notes to practice hearing, seeing, and knowing God in new, creative ways to help you grow in your faith. My prayer is that this book guides you onto a path of seeking, searching, and encountering the Kingdom of Heaven like never before. I want you to know you are invited to encounter Jesus, the Son of the Living God, and meet the Holy Spirit. Each follower of Jesus has an identity and purpose to be found. Let this be your own quest to find your blueprints. These are three ways to talk to God and receive from Him in return. We serve a creative God who speaks in many different languages. We just have to practice translating. You are never too old to learn a new language.

"I am the true grapevine, and my Father is the gardener. He cuts off every branch of mine that doesn't produce fruit, and he prunes the branches that do bear fruit so they will produce even more. You have already been pruned and purified by the message I have given you. Remain in me, and I will remain in you. For a branch cannot produce fruit if it is severed from the vine, and you cannot be fruitful unless you remain in me. Yes, I am the vine; you are the branches. Those who remain in me, and I in them, will produce much fruit. For apart from me you can do nothing. Anyone who does not remain in me is thrown away like a useless branch and withers. Such branches are gathered into a pile to be burned. But if you remain in me and my words remain in you, you may ask for anything you want, and it will be granted! When you produce much fruit, you are my true disciples. This brings great glory to my Father." - John 15:1-8 NLT

 # *Tool 1 – Prayer Guide*

Let Prayer Guide You and Be Your Light

There are many ways God communicates with us as believers. We need to be aware of different ways to go before the King of Kings and receive His divine instructions.

"But all who listen to me will live in peace, untroubled by fear of harm."
- Proverbs 1:33 NLT

One way to hear the voice of God is through prayer. We can do all the "right" things, like going to church and taking Bible classes, but we cannot have a third-person relationship with Jesus Christ. He desires to be our best friend, and how can He be your friend if you don't talk to Him?

"Taste and see that the Lord is good. Oh, the joys of those who take refuge in Him!" - Psalm 34:8 NLT

Taste Him for yourself. Engage in conversation with Him in order to test and know His character for yourself. He wants you to experience that He really is all that is said of Him. Think about a new cool kid coming into your class and how people can tell you all about that person, but until you meet Him personally and start hanging out and having conversations, He isn't your friend. He might want to be, but until you engage personally, He is simply an acquaintance at best. The integrity of our relationship with Jesus Christ needs to be guarded in a way that in a day where many false prophets will rise, we can rely on our relationship with Christ Jesus to separate ourselves from the false.

"Listen to me, you who know right from wrong, you who cherish my law in your hearts. Do not be afraid of people's scorn, nor fear their insults."

- Isaiah 51:7 NLT

We also don't want to find ourselves operating out of witchcraft or a fortune teller's heart. Our desire should be to follow the example of Jesus to speak only what our Father is speaking and do only what the Father is instructing. How can we know what He is doing and saying without spending time in His presence and engaging in a relationship with Him? Some examples of Scriptures revealing the difference between God and the abuse of His name without a relationship with Him include the stories referenced in Acts 19:13-19, Acts 16:16-18, and Acts 8:9-24. In Moses's Day, the Egyptian Pharaoh had magicians who could copy some of the same miracles God performed through Moses, as in Exodus 7:11, 22. One of my favorite stories about the integrity of our words can be found in Numbers chapter 22.

In my personal intimacy with Christ Jesus, I was led by the Holy Spirit to write out a prayer guide. It's for anyone trying to see change and desiring a closer relationship. This is simply an outline example that I felt compelled to write. It is certainly not the only way to pray, just an example of one that has helped me release the presence of God. I pray this guide and my testimony will lead you to Tiffany. I pray it will be a guide to practice intimacy.

You can view it as one prayer or you can pray any section you feel compelled to pray independently.

"Enter His gates with thanksgiving; go into His courts with praise. Give thanks to Him and praise His name." - **Psalm 100:4 NLT**

Personally, that's exactly where I am seeking to go—into His heavenly courts. After Thanksgiving, I looked at the Lord's Prayer in Matthew 6:9-13 and considered the segments. When we pray this way, I believe we agree with God's blueprints for our lives to manifest themselves. We must be led by Christ's example. I encourage you to pray often as the example in Matthew 7:7-11 teaches us that when we continue to seek and ask for good things of the Kingdom of God, they will be granted. Pray when alone and pray in a group. Matthew 18:19-20 teaches if two agree and ask in the name of Jesus for the will of heaven He will do it.

 PAUSE

I feel in this moment to prepare your heart to receive healing through forgiveness.

Scripture Reference

Genesis 41:51

Lord,

Erase emotional pain caused by traumatic life circumstances and events, just like you erased Joseph's trauma and replaced his heart. I forgive anyone who was manipulated by Satan, falling into his schemes to bring darkness into my life. I also forgive myself for every situation I allowed Satan to use me to bring darkness into others' lives.

In Jesus' Name,

Amen.

Additional Reference:

YouTube A Christmas Prayer in the Mountains Sara George's Love Notes from Heaven: https://www.youtube.com/watch?v=A8V5g0LHUFo

Scripture Reference

1 Chronicles 16:11-12, Psalm 25:4, Proverbs 25:2, Luke 11:34-35, Philippians 3:1-2, Luke 11:52, Philippians 2:3, Luke 11:42-43, Psalm 24:4, Psalm 96:8, Psalm 51, Luke 7:36-50

Lord,

Let the cry of my heart be Psalm 24:4 to come before You with clean hands and a pure heart.

Cleanse me once more. Let me not be so comfortable that I forget to offer you hospitality. Let me not become proud and assume my hands are clean. I don't want to think because I am in a relationship with you, I no longer need cleansing. Bring me higher and let me see deeper into the crevices. Wash me with your words. Let me have a new revelation of who you are so that I can honor and love you more, just as the woman who honored you with her tears and kisses. Let me not grow too complacent that I forget the sacrifice you made because my human goodness cannot compare to yours. I cannot come to righteousness on my own. Let me not be like Saul of Tarsus, full of judgment and hate, but instead like Paul, full of love and mercy for all I encounter. Let me seek your cleansing so I have a deeper revelation and ability to love you and others more. Continue to wash me until everything that hinders my flesh from receiving your love and intimacy is removed.

Remind me of how compromise is like the leaven you spoke of. It taints the whole batch of dough. Instead, let me recognize the spirit of religion when we see and hear hypocrisy. Let our lives be a true, pure witness untainted and holy before you.

Let me always speak in the spirit and seek out your clues like a detective finding the trail of love and mercy left behind for us to follow and witness. Let your fruit be seen like grapes on a sidewalk.

Teach me the difference between identity and pride so we do not mistake truth for arrogance. Remind me opinions hold no revelation or light and can contaminate your perfect witness. Let me choose silence over speaking in human wisdom or opinion. Let me choose the floor over the stage. Let me look into the eyes of individuals instead of over the heads of a crowd. Remind me, we all eat at the same table. As we sit at the table, not one will rise above the other; instead, we show each other mutual honor, love, and respect.

Let not a moment of time be spent in challenging theology and opinion. Instead, remind me that any time spent in a debate is lost time. Let us seek your heart independently over all questions, asking for your truth and counsel. Then, let us trust you enough to know the Holy Spirit can bring me into the light. He will bring light and truth to others without my help, keeping me free of the sin of gossip and slander. You are more than capable of revealing the truth to anyone seeking truth without my help and influence.

Let us see You in every day and every season.

In Jesus' Name,

Amen.

 **UNPAUSE**

And may the Lord, our God, show us His approval and make our efforts successful. Yes, make our efforts successful! **-Psalm 90:17 NLT**

"Seek the Lord while you can find Him. Call on Him now while He is near."

- *Isaiah 55:6 NLT* .

If you have received your prayer language, ignite your spirit man first with your gift of tongues, then start the prayer starter in your native tongue. Pause at the end of each segment and again pray in the spirit and remember to pause and expect to hear a response to your prayer. I encourage you not to rush through the prayer but instead to linger, waiting for the presence and response of God.

Prayer Guide for Growth in Intimacy

Thanksgiving

Additional Reference:

YouTube *Journey into the Presence of God Part 2 Sara George's Love Notes from Heaven*: https://www.youtube.com/watch?v=jp9bQjYJ-qI

Heavenly Father,

Thank You for Your grace and mercy. Thank You for the breath in my lungs so I can sing praises to You. Thank You for coming to receive me. Thank You for taking my sins on the cross. Thank You for my home and family. Thank You for giving me hope and opportunities to serve You as I grow. God, You are my El Roi (The God Who Sees Me), Jehovah-Nissi (My Banner), Ori (My Light), my Shepherd, and my Abba (Father). Thank You for leading me with Your Spirit and prioritizing my daily tasks. Thank You for being concerned with the smallest details.

In Jesus Name,

Amen.

[Continue thanking Him as the Holy Spirit leads you.]

Adoration and Admiration

(This is an example of adoration. I like to start with wisdom. You can certainly pick for yourself, but for me personally, I want to consistently seek His wisdom for and over my life.)

Scripture References

Psalm 90:12, 14, Isaiah 11:2, 1 Corinthians 2:5, 7-12, Isaiah 55:8-9, Daniel 9:4, Psalm 119:34, 66, 68, 73, Exodus 33:13, Proverbs 2:1-12, Proverbs 3:13-20

Father,

Your wisdom is greater than I can imagine. You are wiser than any human's understanding and wiser than the wisest wise man who has walked the Earth. Teach me wisdom in all situations by leading and prompting me with the Holy Spirit. I want to understand Your ways. Show me like You showed Moses so that I can understand You more fully. I want to see and understand Your truth in my life and within others. Let revelation and knowledge create new joy in my life.

In Jesus Name,

Amen.

[Continue admiration and adoration as the Holy Spirit leads you.]

Repentance/Discipline/Purification

Scripture References

Mark 7:21, Romans 5:1-2, Matthew 18:21-22, Isaiah 55:7,
Hebrews 12:5-12, Hebrews 12:15, Psalm 119:75, Proverbs 3:11-12,
Jeremiah 10:23, Malachi 3:3, Zechariah 13:9, Isaiah 55:3, 11,
Numbers 14:22, Isaiah 51:7

"I know, Lord, that our lives are not our own. We are not able to plan our own course. So correct me, Lord, but please be gentle. Do not correct me in anger, for I would die." – Jeremiah 10:23-24 NLT

"How can I know all the sins lurking in my heart? Cleanse me from these hidden faults. Keep your servant from deliberate sins! Don't let them control me. Then I will be free of guilt and innocent of great sin." - Psalm 19:12-13 NLT

Cleanse and purify my heart, Oh Lord. Purify my heart as You purify silver and gold in the fire. Remind me of what You did on the cross. Let Your Holiness convict my heart and show me areas of my life I need to surrender unto You. Please forgive me for any places I have not allowed forgiveness to consume my heart.

Show me who I need to forgive. Take away any bitterness or offense and replace it with your supernatural love. Take any bitterness I have harbored, cleanse me, and make me whole in your eyes. Remind me that when I choose to forgive, I should not hold any condemnation but instead completely forget the offense the way you have forgiven me.

Love

Scripture References

1 Corinthians Chapter 13, Matthew 13:16, Psalm 90:14, Psalm 91:14, 1 John 4:17, 1 John 4:19-21, 1 John 4:7-12, 1 Timothy 1:5, Colossians 3:14, Psalm 63, Ephesians 3:14-19, John 5:20, 1 Thessalonians 3:12-13, 2 Thessalonians 3:5, 1 Peter 1:22, Philippians 1:9-11, 2:1, Romans 8:28, Romans 5:5

Love is the proof you are a follower of Christ. It is the key to unlocking the Kingdom of God in your life. Love strengthens your heart in holiness. When love is uncovered throughout your life and is the byproduct of every spiritual gift, it is the fulfillment of becoming a mature believer in Christ. In all circumstances, let our emotions and reactions be manifestations of the love of heaven being released into the earth.

"And this hope will not lead to disappointment. For we know how dearly God loves us because he has given us the Holy Spirit to fill our hearts with his love." **-Romans 5:5 NLT**

Don't just pretend to love others. Really love them. Hate what is wrong. Hold tightly to what is good. **- Romans 12:9 NLT**

So now I am giving you a new commandment: Love each other. Just as I have loved you, you should love each other. Your love for one another will prove to the world that you are my disciples. **-John 13:34-35 NLT**

Holy Spirit,

Fill my heart with God's love. Teach me to love You the way I am loved so that I can receive all that You have created for me to do and to become. Purify my flesh through the discipline of obedience so that I can make room for Your love. Teach me how to be closer to Your heart so that I may be overflowing with love. Give me Your eyes to see people the way You see them. Teach me to love with Your love. Show me the people You want me to love. Allow me to experience Your supernatural love that can only be from You. Let me be led by love in advancing Your Kingdom. Let me hear with Your ears so I can carry Your love to anyone hurting and searching for You. Mature me into a place of intimacy to release Your love even within difficult situations. Let Your love deliver victory. Through Your grace, let love empower me and be the evidence and proof that I am Yours and You are mine.

In Jesus Name,

Amen.

[Continue as the Holy Spirit leads you.]

SARA C GEORGE

Strategy and Behavior

Scripture References

Job 26:4, Matthew 6:33, Isaiah 11:3-5, 1 John 4:6-7, Psalm 119:73

Father,

Align my heart to change the way I think, feel, and react in all situations with those You have placed in my path and show me the opportunity to demonstrate the fruit of self-control through my example.

Help me to control my emotions and reactions by giving me the mind of Christ. Allow me to see and understand the strategy of the enemy and identify the enemy within situations. Teach me not to hold offense or judgment. Instead, give me discernment to separate the situation from the person, granting clarity and understanding. Help me understand when I look at someone with my flesh, I will find the flesh and faults of others, and when I choose to open my eyes to see in the spirit, I will encounter the position of the person's heart. Show me how to look for the fruit on the tree so I will be able to test and see if it is bitter or sweet. Help me to demonstrate the same polite, gentle nature as the Holy Spirit in my conversations and ways. Remind me the Holy Spirit is not pushy or forceful and doesn't give me things I am not seeking or asking to receive.

In Jesus Name,

Amen.

[Continue as the Holy Spirit leads you.]

Be The Example

Scripture References

Matthew 7:16-19, Genesis 41:38, Psalm 119:74, Psalm 119:34, Acts 4:13, 1 Chronicles 4:9-10

Holy Spirit,

Help me not to compromise or prostitute the Gospel. Guide me to be a person of integrity in word and deed. Let it be spoken that I am so full of the Spirit of God that I look like my Heavenly Father. Allow me to be recognized as someone who has been with Jesus. Lead me to be Your hands and feet wherever I go and with all people. Help me to cause no harm or conflict with others. I give You permission to guide my words and allow me to be Your voice. I will be the instrument, and You can blow through me, taking control of my voice and bridling my tongue. Help me not to tempt or provoke others into bad behavior or actions. Let my example set me apart and lead them into Your love. Help me to stand boldly against conversations that do not honor You. Help me not to be afraid of what other people might think or say when I stand up for righteous behavior and pure conversation. I don't want to pass a single opportunity to be Your witness and observe Your great supernatural intervention into the lives of all those I encounter. You are Elohim.

In Jesus Name,

Amen.

[*Continue as the Holy Spirit leads you.*]

Honor

Love each other with genuine affection, and take delight in honoring each other.

- Romans 12:10 NLT

Father,

I want to honor You with what I watch, listen to, and consume. Show me and convict me anytime I am outside of Your will for my life. Show me how to honor others with my words and actions. Let me stay teachable, removing pride and rebellion from my heart. Don't let the world be my measure of worth; instead, align my life with Your perfect will each and every day.

In Jesus Name,

Amen.

[Continue as the Holy Spirit leads you.]

Respect My Position/Fear of the Lord

Scripture References

Exodus 14:14, Psalm 23, Psalm 91, Matthew 7:2, Matthew 18:33, Matthew 23:8-12, Psalm 90:16, Psalm 90:11, Psalm 91:11-12, Isaiah 11:2, 1 Corinthians 3:5-9, Mark 9:35, Isaiah 54:17, Hebrews 12:28-29, Psalm 119:38, Psalm 49:15, Psalm 50:6, Proverbs 1:7, Psalm 44:5, 7, Psalm 54:1-2, 5; Psalm 55:9, 16-18

Abba,

Teach me what it means to fear the Lord. Let me understand what it means to tremble before You. I want to have revelation to comprehend Your authority and power. Allow me to seek You, and as I learn, give me Your blessing and favor. Position my heart in humility like that of a servant. Send your angels to protect and guard me. Remind me that You are my Defender, and I do not need to judge or punish anyone, especially those you have given me to love. You are strong enough and do not need my assistance or help in any way. Help me pray, seek, and love the way You command. Allow me to experience Your vindication by becoming a servant of the Most High God.

In Jesus Name,

Amen.

[Continue as the Holy Spirit leads you.]

Tool 2 – Activation

Activate and Navigate Growth

This is a visual activation tool to pray through and engage your spirit by igniting your spiritual senses. Another way God likes to communicate is visually. He can give you dreams, visions, or simple pictures of words or instructions imprinted into your imagination. This is a simple fiction story using a creative story telling technique to help you engage your five senses. The story and the prayer starter have some similarities and intertwine. It is not intended to replace or expand on the Holy Bible; however, scripture is noted throughout the story which gives inspiration in the fictional story.

In the spring of 2020, I had a dream about going on a canoe trip that inspired "The Journey." In the dream, I was going to the river with people who thought they were ready to float down the river straight out of the car. I wasn't ready yet. I wanted to go inside the cabin and eat a meal before I floated down river. I was hungry and went inside by myself and ordered a four-course meal. I took my time eating and didn't go out until I was full. When I went back outside, everyone had left, and I found myself alone. It was dusk, and I was wondering why it was so late. I wondered how long I was inside eating. It was the evening, and I didn't really want to go canoeing in the dark alone. I tried to make a phone call with a pay phone, which seems odd in our modern time. I watched myself try to make a call, but it was very short, and I didn't reach anyone. Perhaps I realized that there wasn't anyone to call, or maybe that the old payphone no longer worked. I also felt that there wasn't anyone to call because the ones who I would have called had already left. I decided there wasn't anyone to come to pick me up and my only option was to get in a canoe. Thinking about the dream I realize it's odd that I felt I couldn't drive myself home. I came to the river in a car, but there was some reason I could not leave the same way I came. I was nervous about going because of the wooded landscape, and I heard sounds in the distance, but I got in the boat. The darkness caused fear to try to take hold of me, and I felt intimidated. I knew I was safe on the boat, so I pushed out into the water. I knew Jesus was with me, and I had to stay with Jesus. I felt that it was a visual interpretation of Psalm 23. Like many dreams, I don't remember the entire dream or how it ended; I just remember being with Jesus and knowing if I was right behind him, I was safe. It is the idea or theme God revealed for the short story "The Journey" because we will be in these dark places at times where we need to be instructed and protected by the Lord. This short story will guide you on how to receive clarity in turbulent times.

 **PAUSE**

Let's stop for a moment and pray this small prayer from my journal to prepare our hearts for "The Journey".

Father,

Thank You, Jesus, for preparing a place for me and protecting me on the journey. Thank You for blessing your people as radiant ones. Unseal our lips, O Lord! Let us be Your mouthpiece, for we belong to You. Let us speak only what is true and declare what is right. Teach us how to bind and loose. Show us the right way to use Your keys. Honor us by allowing us to worship You. Teach us how to rest and prepare. Thank You for being my Father, Mother, and Friend. Forgive us. Discipline us but be gentle. Purify our hearts and align us for Your great purpose and plan.

Release our destiny scroll of what You have written and planned for our future so we can agree and fulfill all You have for our lives.

Teach us to guard our time. Holy Spirit, show us areas where distraction, procrastination, rebellion, and witchcraft have found legal ground in our lives so that we may repent and cover ourselves in Jesus' unlimited merciful sacrifice. Bind the spirits of distraction, procrastination, rebellion, and witchcraft in Jesus' name.

Let us not lean right or left, but instead, stay in perfect unison step behind You. Teach us not to compare our assignments to others. Instead, let us be passionately dedicated to You.

Remind us we wear the helmet of salvation. Show me that the only path I see wearing a helmet is straight ahead. I cannot be distracted if my eyes are fixed on You. It's only when I turn my neck and take my eyes off You that I am lured into distraction, jealousy, and false motives. Teach me to keep my eyes focused on You.

I want to be a witness to Your Supernatural Kingdom. Display Your power and make Yourself famous once more. Give me opportunities to testify to Your great healing power and love. Examine my heart and see if my motivation is pure. Remove anything that offends or defiles You. If my heart deceives me in any way, please purify it once more until only gold remains. Let me reflect on Your image, ways, love, and beauty. Let me be so full of Your Holy Spirit that anyone who passes my way sees You instead of my flesh.

Teach us how You want to be remembered. Show us how to stay close to You in the land of plenty. Teach us how to sit at Your feet even in the blessings. Continue to purify and sift our hearts, increasing our understanding of the fear of the Lord so that we may honor You in all Your ways. Remove pride and religion from our culture, replacing it with love, compassion, and mercy for all people. Send Your angels to guard our homes.

Let us not forget the name of Jesus in all we do and speak. Instead, may we give Him acknowledgment in every movement and word. Remind us Jesus is in us and with us. In every step and experience, let us trust and obey while You fight off all doubt and fear that hinders our way.

In Jesus' Name,

Amen.

JOURNEY

Additional Reference:

YouTube Journey Into the Presence of God Part 4 Sara George's Love Notes from Heaven: https://www.youtube.com/watch?v=_sORLnowXx4

If reading the story aloud to a group, I recommend you ask the audience to remain as quiet and still as possible during the reading to avoid distracting those around them. I also recommend passing out paper and pens for journaling throughout the journey. Some people focus better visually if they close their eyes. I have set apart the read-aloud portion by increasing the font size to make it stand out. The other portions are additional scripture references and further explanations for reviewing the story independently. Allow yourself moments to pause, listen, and linger throughout the story.

This is an encounter opportunity. Partner with the Holy Spirit and let these words activate your five senses. Visualize yourself in the story. What do you see, hear, and smell? Take notes and allow yourself to become a participant, the main character, not just a spectator observing. We are all main characters and not the supporting actors. We each have our own scroll where we are in the lead role.

Our Father is a fountain of Living Water. He welcomes us and makes us new and different by refreshing and rejuvenating our minds, bodies, and souls when we enter His presence. My prayer is that this activation story will rejuvenate and refresh every part of you as you choose to partner and participate with the Holy Spirit.

"The Lord will guide you continually, giving you water when you are dry and restoring your strength. You will be like a well-watered garden, like an ever-flowing spring." -Isaiah 58:11 NLT

The fountain is representative of the Holy Spirit. Throughout history and in many modern churches, we have relied on the traditions of the church and a pastor in a pulpit to try to fill our cisterns. When we try to fill them ourselves without going to the fountain, we are forsaking God the Father. Cisterns like these are broken and cannot hold water.

"For my people have done two evil things: They have abandoned me—the fountain of living water. And they have dug for themselves cracked cisterns that can hold no water at all!" -Jeremiah 2:13 NLT

Instead, we should seek the baptism of fire through receiving the Holy Spirit. When the Holy Spirit fills our well and dwells inside us, instead of us just going into the church building for a drink, we become a fountain and can take the Holy Spirit with us, and God will provide the Spirit in an endless supply.

Let's set the stage. I want to guide you visually with my words so that you can start to get a visual representation of going into the presence of the Lord. I will give you a multi-dimensional road so that it will become as helpful as possible to get to a place where you can listen and receive instructions visually from our ABBA Father.

"Your instructions are more valuable to me than millions in gold and silver."

-Psalm 119:72 NLT

Use your senses of sight, touch, smell, sound, and taste as we journey together. The image I'm receiving to share is a small boat with only room for two. I imagine a canoe or gondola with Jesus standing as your guide. Visualize a beautiful, gentle river of flowing water. Listen, can you hear the flowing water? This water is perfect because it flows from the heart of God to the Heavenly City. I imagine a beautiful waterfall flowing down from Heaven into a smooth river to reach you right where you are. Next, take in the smells of the fresh air all around you and feel a gentle breeze.

"A river brings joy to the city of our God, the sacred home of the Most High. God dwells in that city; it cannot be destroyed. From the very break of day, God will protect it." **-Psalm 46:4-5 NLT**

"Then the angel showed me a river with the water of life, clear as crystal, flowing from the throne room of God and of the Lamb. It flowed down the center of the main street."- **Revelation 22:1-2 NLT**

"The king's heart is like a stream of water directed by the Lord; he guides it wherever he pleases."- **Proverbs 21:1 NLT**

"O God, You are my God; I earnestly search for you. My soul thirsts for you; my whole body longs for you in this parched and weary land where there is no water."- **Psalm 63:1 NLT**

"I lie awake thinking of you, meditating on you through the night."

- Psalm 63:6 NLT

Seek out songs that remind you of a need and a desire for intimacy with our Creator God, Elohim, and His Son Jesus.

Imagine you are standing on the riverbank waiting to see His boat pull up to you. What are the sounds your ears are drawn towards? Do you smell a sweet aroma? What do you feel? Start calling out to Him. He is in the distance. Thank Him for all He is and does for His people.

"Let all that I am wait quietly before God, for my hope is in Him."

-Psalm 62:5 NLT

*"Be still, and know that I am God! I will be honored by every nation. I will be honored throughout the world." - **Psalm 46:10 NLT***

Cry out, "Where are you, Abba?" And you will hear His response like osmosis into your heart. He will say, "I am right here."

*"My heart has heard you say, 'Come and talk with me.' And my heart responds, "Lord, I am coming.'"- **Psalm 27:8 NLT***

I see Father's hand reaching out as He guides me into the boat. I feel His strength and gentleness lift me up into His safety. As I enter the boat and as He starts to paddle, I see a bend in the river. At the bend, I look out on the shore and see a moment in time past. It is at the foot of the cross where my El Yeshuati (Savior) won the victory, giving me access to have a relationship with His Father, Abba. Visualize the scene standing before you. I see the cross on a hill with my Lord hanging, unrecognizable by His broken flesh and spilled blood. I smell the stench of rotting flesh and infection in the hot sun. I hear the crowd mocking, screaming, and howling. I hear and feel the buzzing flies and bugs being drawn to the carcasses.

(Suggestion- Take communion as you visualize going under the cross.)

As we curve around the bend, we go straight under the cross, and I hear and feel the precious blood of my Lord as it drips down the cross and is sprinkled on me as I pass beneath Him. By trust and faith in Him and through our acceptance of His sacrifice, we receive salvation. When we receive salvation, the Holy Spirit has access to our lives. He writes His laws on our minds and hearts, so we know right from wrong by access to the Holy Spirit. When we desire more of God and cry out to have the Holy Spirit consume our earthly bodies, we become filled with His Spirit from our toes to the top of our heads. The Holy Spirit will gently lead and guide you into a transformation, becoming a new creation in Christ Jesus from the inside out. The Holy Spirit leads you to a life with conviction and trains you to become holy, righteous, and pure. He will draw you to quick conviction when you make mistakes. He remembers how fragile we can be and that we are made from dust.

"...Because of Christ and our faith in Him, we can now come boldly and confidently into God's presence." -Ephesians 3:12 NLT

"Let us go right into the presence of God with sincere hearts fully trusting Him. For our guilty consciences have been sprinkled with Christ's blood to make us clean, and our bodies have been washed with pure water."

-Hebrews 10:22 NLT

As the float continues, I see a heavenly city start to appear in the distance. The city has a great wall around it and a mountain below it. There is a gap between the mountain and the city with what looks like fog between them, but then I notice the smoke billowing out of my Savior's nostrils. I imagine a heavenly escalator or portal moving angels and believers up through the smoke into the heavenly city. The river approaches the city walls. I understand I can get to the wall of the city through my acceptance and relationship with Jesus, and I see a gate leading deeper into the city.

At the city wall, the atmosphere changes, and you start to feel supernatural love, joy, and peace. I hear Yeshua's heart calling for thanksgiving, praise, and worship. I hear a symphony of praise coming from all directions. I cannot make out the words, but it is harmonizing into sounds that melt into its own language. The gates open for my boat and my Advocate (Parakletos). I start to fix my thoughts and eyes in front of me, seeking and searching for my Abba. I know that the gates open for me because of the sincerity and desire of my heart to follow the promptings of the Holy Spirit into righteousness and holiness by allowing myself to be consumed and transformed with a complete filling of the Holy Spirit.

"Open for me the gates where the righteous enter, and I will go in and thank the Lord. These gates lead to the presence of the Lord, and the godly enter there. I thank you for answering my prayer and giving me victory!"

-Psalm 118:19-21 NLT

"Our city is strong! We are surrounded by the walls of God's salvation. Open the gates to all who are righteous; allow the faithful to enter. You will keep in perfect peace all who trust in you, all whose thoughts are fixed on you!"

-Isaiah 26:1-3 NLT

"Who may climb the mountain of the Lord? Who may stand in His holy place? Only those whose hands and hearts are pure, who do not worship idols and never tell lies. They will receive the Lord's blessing and have a right relationship with God their Savior. Such people may seek you and worship in your presence, O God of Jacob." -Psalm 24:3-6 NLT

"You will show me the way of life, granting me the joy of your presence and the pleasures of living with you forever." -Psalm 16:11 NLT

Approaching ahead of me, in a place where the river pools, is an ancient gate. Visualize an ancient gate. What do you think it looks like? What do you see? I imagine I am already within a walled city, but the river has taken me deeper into the heart of the city, where I see a castle with an inner wall. It is like a grand castle drawbridge gate door: tall, heavy, and thick. I imagine reaching out and feeling the rough wood and depth of the layer leading into the castle. What do you hear? I hear the squeaking pulley operating the gate as it opens for Jesus and me.

I exit the boat and walk a path to an ancient door. The ancient door stands tall and wide. I hear it creaking open. My mouth opens, and I hear a love song coming forth from deep within me. The ancient door opens, and I feel compelled to offer up my heart and life as a sacrifice to my Lord as the King of Glory takes His seat on a throne before me. At the moment, nothing matters. I have no thoughts in my mind. I see the light radiating and exploding around me. I feel words in my spirit saying, "What can I do for you, Lord? How can I serve you?" What do you see? What do you hear? Can you imagine His face in front of you? Do you see yourself bowed on your knees, face to the floor in worship, and all the while feeling and knowing His presence is all around you, encompassing you completely?

Picture His face and fix your thoughts on Him. I sense a rushing coolness rejuvenating my soul as His living water pours over me. His presence restores and refreshes my spirit, soul, and mind. He restores my strength. I feel light as if I am made of helium and might float away. You will feel supernatural love, joy, protection, and peace in His presence as He responds. I feel it inside my heart. He says, "Let me teach you what to ask to make you strong."

"Those who live in the shelter of the Most High will find rest in the shadow of the Almighty. This I declare about the Lord: He alone is my refuge, my place of safety; He is my God, and I trust Him." -**Psalm 91:1-2 NLT**

"You hide them in the shelter of your presence, safe from those who conspire against them. You shelter them in your presence, far from accusing tongues."

-**Psalm 31:20 NLT**

"Open up, ancient gates! Open up, ancient doors, and let the King of Glory enter. Who is the King of Glory? The Lord, strong and mighty; the Lord invincible in battle. Open up, ancient gates, open up, ancient doors, and let the King of Glory enter. Who is the King of Glory? The Lord of Heaven's Armies, He is the King of Glory." -**Psalm 24:7-10 NLT**

 PAUSE

Pause to pray and listen. I recommend journaling what you hear.

 **UNPAUSE**

Allow your mind to be open and free to receive the response He has for you. He can read your thoughts and heart discerning if your motives are pure. Anyone seeking Him will find Him, and He will respond, "Yes, my son or daughter." He will bless, refresh, replenish, encourage, and motivate. He will give you detailed instructions. He will fill your heart with His desires and plans.

Picture His face. Fix your thoughts on waiting for His response. What do you see? What do you hear? What do you feel? I imagine returning to the boat and floating with Jesus while I wait because my Father is slow to speak, using wisdom and simplicity in His response. Sometimes, He speaks only one or two words.

I hear the calm water gurgling, I hear beautiful string instruments and trumpets, and there are birds and fish jumping in the river playing in the distance. I can smell a sweet, beautiful floral fragrance. I feel the freedom in the light atmosphere. I feel a gentle breeze and a splash of cool water. I see a tall snow-capped mountain in the distance. I see color as if it were more vibrant, showing me that on Earth, there is a covering of ash disguising the true nature of color. We pull into the next bend of the river, and I see a table prepared before me. I have been invited to dine with the King of Glory as an honored guest. I exit the boat, and I am received by my ancestors and prophets of old. I feel their love, joy, and excitement as I enter the dining room.

Therefore, since we are surrounded by such a huge crowd of witnesses to the *life of faith, let us strip off every weight that slows us down, especially the sin that so easily trips us up. And let us run with endurance the race God has set before us. We do this by keeping our eyes on Jesus, the champion who initiates and perfects our faith. - **Hebrews 12:1-2 NLT.***

The dining room consists of two sections: a formal dining area and a separate patio room set up with more casual coffee-house-style round tables for two. I take my seat in the casual dining room at a table set for two, but there are many tables. There is a table so long your eyes cannot see the end in either direction. There are names on every chair. Some of the chairs are empty. Some people are sitting on the ground near their chairs but have not yet taken their seats in the heavenly realm. Perhaps it still feels out of reach, or they feel unworthy of the position, but I hear the Father sweetly echoing, "ARISE my child and take your seat."

PAUSE

Stop, pray, and listen. Can you hear your name? They are calling you up higher. Pause and check your spiritual senses. What is the aroma, the sound, the feeling, the overall impression you receive?

UNPAUSE

I smell fresh bread. I hear the tinkle of crystal and china. I can hear a beautiful melody at a low volume. Perhaps it is the sounds of the river and the trees singing their songs. I look out a large window and see a glorious light and the crystal sea. I imagine that in heaven, it could be a never-ending sunset, much like parts of Alaska in the summer months. I long for that heavenly view. At the table, the only face I see is Jesus. I understand that it is Jesus in each person who has given their life as a living sacrifice and that Jesus fills every gap and every hole in each one, and at the end of the transformation, you see Jesus reflected in each child of God. I see my name written on the back of a chair in the main dining area and my name on a place card on the patio table. My Father has joined me from His throne to the table to dine with me. My Father comes over and gently kisses my head and anoints my head with oil. My head tilts back, and I open my mouth as an angel pours wine, not into a glass, but into me. Abba gives the instructions. The menu is a selection of Scripture, revelations, and promises. I am told to eat until I am full. I listen quietly while I consume what appears to be books. I stay until I have had a full four-course meal. I see Jesus, my Beloved Brother, waiting to reach out for my hand.

Let's continue deeper into the city chambers. The next stop is the garden. Let's imagine the gardens in heaven together. I see many gardens. I hear the birds and smell the roses. There is such a sweet, fresh fragrance in the air. "I created you in your mother's womb and I can hear your sound like an individual vibration. Just like the birds, you have a song. As I pass by, my beauty brings music from every living creature, big or small. I get joy in the morning visiting my creations. I wake up the Earth with a breath and a song. I smile and laugh every time creation hears my songs and echoes back to me with their own individual melody. I absorb each one as a vibration of energy. Do you hear the sounds I make for you?" Jesus holds out His hand and asks me for a key. It is an old iron key, but it's mine.

Jesus needs my permission to open the door and enter my garden. I hear Him say, "You are a good friend, and I am uniquely captivated by you. Your heart is mesmerizing to me. I am satisfied with all you do, and I love you, but now let me restore your heart. I'm cutting away everything that's dead or dying to make room for new growth in this season. Be still as I gently pluck you out and separate you. Wait patiently while I make room for your growth. I will tie you to a stake to keep you stable as your fruit becomes heavy in this season."

The garden represents our heart. I feel the weight of the key in my hand and see the craftsmanship in the precision of the engraving on its edges. As we approach a hidden door, I hand Him the key, and as I do, I release weight as the iron is removed from my fingers. It's a beautiful door made of wood and rounded off across the top. I am anticipating the beauty. Instead, the place I thought was ready and waiting is something unexpected. It appears as if it has been locked up and abandoned for too long. I am unprepared for the view. It is a tangled mess of vines and weeds. I start to cry with the work set before me. I understand each vine and weed represents a lie I believed or a false teaching. Jesus lifts my chin and wipes my tears. He then takes my hand and lifts me up to a higher place on a mountain, stretching higher to the place of the eagle's nest. I see a set of binoculars like you might find on a scenic overlook or lookout tower. When I look through the new lens, I can see with His eyes, the Eyes of the Father. I see what is under the vines and weeds. It is a majestic, kingly courtyard. There are roses of every color in full bloom. The pattern and design of the garden is idyllic. In the center, I see a three-tier fountain with a river of living water as its source. The fountain represents the Holy Spirit Baptism. It gurgles and cycles, flowing in and out, bringing refreshing life. There is a tree with a low thick branch perfect for a swing or as a seat by itself. I see many animals and pets ready to greet me. Jesus explains what I am looking at is under the vines and debris. He tells me that the roses represent the people who were brought into the Kingdom of God through the garden gate of my heart. There are so many different ones. I am in awe that He could use me to make a difference in the population of heaven.

I fall to His feet and begin to cry out, "I am not worthy, and Holy, Holy, Holy is the Lord God Almighty."

This time, He speaks, saying, "Now, are you willing to help me pull out those vines and weeds so your garden will be uncovered?"

I respond with rejuvenation, enthusiasm, and renewed energy, "YES, I am ready to work. Where do I start? Show me where I have stony, calloused places in my heart. Take my heart and replace and renew every dry, scarred place. Turn it into a pliable substance that moves and flexes."

He says, "Don't worry. I will help you uproot every vine and weed that doesn't belong. Every struggle in the sun, 'son,' will be worth the effort. Watch your step, stay focused, and listen to my voice. There is great grace for you as you grow into my heart. Let me restore you. As you walk through the garden, I will guide you through turbulent waters, restoring your health and beauty. Search for me, and I will show up in the deep places as you uncover the lies and false teachings of your youth. Remember, you are in the garden now. It's a root season to rest and grow as I prepare to send you out. Sit in the fire of My Presence and watch as everything changes. Be still and wait while I clear the path of debris and danger ahead of you. Sit with me as often as you can, and I will light a fire that cannot be quenched and will burn with an eternal flame. Seek me, and I will blow my breath on the pilot light of your heart, and a wildfire will burn out every weed and vine with an intense fire, moving with such intensity that you will be amazed at the pace of progress. There is a blessing for those that linger. You will see only the ashes behind you as you are unveiled as a beautiful white rose. Listen for My Song to call you out of hiding and back onto the path. I will teach you to separate each sound and discern any echoing or twisting that isn't me. Don't worry, I haven't forgotten you. I am simply searching for where I want to plant you. Soon, you will hear a great symphony of songs all around you as I move people towards you to partner with us in the harvest of the Earth."

If you continue to sit in the quiet and allow the Holy Spirit to draw you, the conversation will continue. You can get back in the canoe and let Him lead you even deeper into His innermost chambers. You can go before His royal courtroom and plead cases as an advocate and intercessor. He might take you back into His dining room and sit you down at a table He has prepared for you. He might take you to the top of a high mountain peak or the Crystal Sea. Enjoy your journey into the presence of God.

Pastor Eddie James

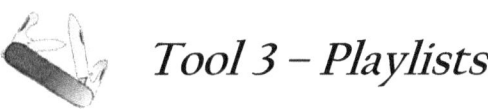 *Tool 3 – Playlists*

Cut Through Darkness

There are times when you will find it easier for you to connect and hear God's voice through music. Here's a sample of some songs I divided into categories that have been instrumental for me on my journey. Some of these categories align to fit the categories represented in the prayer starter and journey story. You can try pausing through each segment of the story below and listening to a song or two from each category. I encourage you to create your own list. Some of these songs could really fit into multiple categories. I feel creating your own lists and your own categories helps your growth. In different seasons it could be different passages of scriptures as your guide. For example, The Lord's Prayer, Psalm 91, or Psalm 23 breaks it down into themes with the help of the Holy Spirit, discovering the layers of categories of songs that fit into the passage.

Calling, Seeking, Searching Songs

- "Holy Spirit" Francesca Battistelli
- "The More I Seek You" Kari Jobe
- "Psalm 63" Emmy Rose Bethel Music
- "Psalm 4 When I Call" The Psalms Project
- "Great Chief Mountain" Worship Rebels
- "In Over My Head" Jenn Johnson
- "Made for More" Josh Baldwin, Jenn Johnson
- "Hunger" David and Nicole Binion
- "Only You" Kim Walker Smith
- "Ghost of a King" The Gray Havens
- "Miracles" Brandon Lake
- "Show me Your Face" Steffany Gretzinger
- "Thy Kingdom Come" Francesca Battistelli and Rita Springer
- "Tongues of Fire" Luke Partridge
- "Just Want You" Sarah Reeves
- "Give me Jesus" Danny Gokey
- "Give Thanks" Hannah Hobbs
- "I Need a Ghost" Brandon Lake
- "I Thank God" Catherine Mullins

- "Oh How I Long For You" Barrett House Productions

- "Take Me In" Catherine Mullins

- "Run to the Father" Cody Carnes, Kari Jobe

- "Spirit Lead Me" Michael Ketterer

- "I Want to Know You" Jeremy Riddle

- "Take Me There" Anna Golden

- "Made For Jesus" John Mark Pantana

- "Psalm 46" Capital City Music

Evalyn Russum

Waiting/Expecting

- "Walk in the Promise" Jeremy Riddle

- "Eyes Locked on the King" Abbie Gamboa

- "Still God" Anna Golden

- "Rest B-Side" John Mark Pantana

- "I Will Wait for You Psalm 130" Shane & Shane

- "Meet Your Maker" John Mark Pantana

- "Wonder in the Waiting" River Crossing

- "The Story I Will Tell" Naomi Raine

- "Watching Over Me" Jason Upton

- "We're Open" Rick Pino

- "On The Banks" Chris Renzema

- "Palm of Your Hand" TRIBL

- "Hymn of the Holy Spirit" Pat Barrett

- "I'm Listening" Chris McClarney

- "Honesty" Elle Limebear

- "Praise Before My Breakthrough" Bryan & Katie Torwalt

- "Give Thanks" Eddie James

- "Just Like in Heaven" Victory Boyd

- "We Need a Miracle" Charity Gayle

- "Goodness" Elle Limebear
- "Burn for You" Rick Pino
- "Housefires" Blake Wiggins & Ahjah Walls
- "Be Still My Soul" Kari Jobe
- "Abide" Aaron Williams
- "Deeper" David & Nicole Binion
- "I Will Wait for You" Shane and Shane
- "Oh How I Long For You" Barrett House Productions
- "Just Be" Kim Walker Smith
- "While I Wait" Lincoln Brewster
- "Rest" Kari Jobe
- "Where Are You" Leeland
- "Gratitude" Brandon Lake
- "Wait on the Lord" James Wilson
- "Don't Be Afraid" Tom Mottershead
- "Rest" John Mark Pantana
- "Be Still" Jeremy Riddle

Admiration/Adoration/Holy Attributes

- "Maker of the Moon" Elle Limelear
- 'I love You Lord" Eddie James
- "Jesus, You're Beautiful" Jason Upton
- "Jesus, You're Beautiful" Jon Thurlow
- "Fairest" UPPERROOM
- "Majesty" Roy Fields
- "Goodness of God" CeCe Winans
- "Lost in Your Love" Brandon Lake
- "Wildflowers" Brandon Lake
- "Worthy of it All" UpperRoom
- "What a Beautiful Name" Victory Boyd
- "Garments of Praise" Isaiah 61 James Block
- "Faithful" Sarah Reeves
- "Do it Again" Elevation Worship
- "My Jesus" Anne Wilson
- "Glorify Thy Name" Jeremy Riddle
- "All Hail King Jesus" Jeremy Riddle
- "Better Than Wine" Jon Thurlow
- "For The Cross" UpperRoom

- "There is a Name" Sean Feucht
- "There's Nothing That Our God Can't Do" Passion Music
- "Your Word is True" Nathan Taylor
- "Your Word is True" Yemi Levite
- "Always Good" Hannah McClure
- "Taste and See" Shane & Shane
- "Taste and See" John Mark Pantana
- "How Great Thou Art" Lauren Diagle
- "How Great is Our God" Josie Buchanan
- "How Great is Our God" Caleb & Kelsey
- "My Favorite" Gideon Roberts & Abbie Simmons
- "Wisdom Song" Laura Woodley Osman
- "Perfect Wisdom of our God" Keith & Kristyn Getty

Repentance/Deliverance/Purification

- "Freedom" Eddie James
- "Warfare" Victory Boyd
- "El Shaddai" Victory Boyd
- "This is Amazing Grace" Lauren Daigle
- "Amazing Grace" Caleb and Kelsey
- "Pure" Abbie Gamboa
- "The Blood" Eddie James
- "Righteous" Victory Boyd
- "Broken Vessels" Sarah Reeves
- "Sword of the Lord" Luke Partridge
- "Song of Deliverance" Zach Williams
- "No Longer Slaves" Bethel Music
- "The Breakup Song" Francesca Battistelli
- "No Fear" Kari Jobe
- "Fires" Jordan St. Cyr
- "Mention of Your Name" Bethel Music
- "Tremble" Jeremy Riddle
- "My Weapon" Natalie Grant
- "Fear is a Liar" Zach Williams

- "I will not Fear" (Elohim Shomri) extended version Yeka Onka Jesus Co & WorshipMob
- "Let It Rain" Eddie James
- "Let It Rain" Michael W Smith
- "Something has to Break" Red Rocks Worship
- "I Say Yes" Kim Walker Smith
- "There is a Fountain" Victory Boyd
- "Purify My Heart" Jeremy Riddle
- "Promise Land" Jonathan & Melissa Hessler
- "Faithful Go and Speak" Amy Grant and Ellie Holcomb
- "Pharoah" Brandon Lake
- "Psalm 23" Jason Upton
- "Breakthrough" Eddie James
- "Sound Mind" Cageless Birds
- "Prepare the Way" Bethel Music, Bethany Wohrle & Dante Bowe
- "Set a Table" Sean Feucht & Steffany Gretzinger
- "He's a Chain Breaker" Zach Williams
- "Refiners Fire" Brian Doerksen & TWP Band
- "Protector" Kim Walker Smith
- "Deliver Me" John Mark MacMillan

- "Freedom is Coming" Young & Free

- "Never Lost" Catherine Mullins

- "Speak the Name" Koryn Hawthorne

- "Break Every Chain" Tasha Cobbs

- "Bye Bye Babylon" Elevation Worship

- "The Sound of Freedom" Cageless Birds

- "The Battle is Yours" Paul Wilbur

- "Giants Fall" Francesca Battistelli

- "Remember" Lauren Daigle

- "If My People" Robby Cummings

Rochelle Tierney

Peace/Entrance to the Heavenly City

- "Behold He is Coming" James Block
- "Turn Your Eyes Upon Jesus" Lauren Daigle
- "There was Jesus" Zach Williams & Dolly Parton
- "Psalm 91" Victory Boyd
- "Eagle's Majestic Flight" Ken Soltys
- "Canticle" TAYA
- "It is Well With my Soul" Anthem Lights
- "Rejoice" Victory Boyd
- 'Ladder" Rick Pino
- "Be Enthroned" Jeremy Riddle
- "Gentle and Lowly" Tom Mottershead
- "Better is One Day" Eddie James
- "Throne Room" Kim Walker Smith
- "Better is One Day" Kim Walker Smith
- "When I Lock Eyes With You" UPPERROOM
- "Here as in Heaven" Matt Gillman
- "His Eye is on the Sparrow" Victory Boyd
- "All Hail King Jesus" Jeremy Riddle
- "Psalm 4 When I Call" – The Psalms Project

- "Holy Ground" Jeremy Riddle

- "Trust in You" - Lauren Daigle

- "Peace" Jason Upton

- "Peace" Anna Golden

- "Firm Foundation" Cody Carnes

- "The Angels and the Elders" Cageless Birds

- "Here as in Heaven" Dajon Cambridge

Dajon Cambridge

Love/Surrender/Sacrifice

- "I Just Love You" Upperroom
- "Your Love" Joy Cone
- "Obedience" Lindy & The Circuit Riders
- "Where You Go I Go" Jenn Johnson, Brian Johnson
- "Nobody Like You" Paul Wilbur Ministries
- "Arms Wide Open" Misty Edwards
- "Gold" Jesus Culture
- "Jesus Over Everything" TAYA
- "Reckless Love" Bethel Music
- "Jesus Have it All" Jeremy Riddle
- "Every Heart" Unveiled Worship
- "I Have Decided" Elevation Worship
- "I Surrender All" Caleb + Kelsey
- "Made to Love You" Dann & Beckie Thompson
- "Pieces" (Spontaneous) Amanda Cook Bethel Music
- "Oh How He Loves You and Me" Eddie James
- "Driven By Love" Lindy & The Circuit Riders
- "Glass Window" Cochren & Co.
- "Heart of God" Capital City Music

- "Here's my Heart" Lauren Daigle
- "Love like This" Lauren Daigle
- "Abraham" Josh Baldwin
- "Jesus Have It All" Jeremy Riddle
- "Send Me" Bethel Music Jenn Johnson
- "Isaiah 6" Lindy Cofer
- "Whatever Your Plan is" Josie Buchanan
- "By Our Love" King & Country
- "Lamb" Tiffany Hudson Elevation Worship
- "Fall Afresh" Sarah Reeves
- "Nothing Else" Cody Carnes
- "Rooftops" Jesus Culture
- "No Higher Praise" Jason Upton
- "Worthy of it All" Anna Dow
- "Changing Me" Anna Golden
- "Love Note" Gabriela Mejia
- "Just want You" The Belonging Co

Response/Answer

- "You Say" Lauren Daigle

- "Open Wide" Cageless Birds

- "Breath of Yah" James Block

- "There in the Middle" Harvest and Jon Thurlow

- "Zion" Aaron Shust

- "If My People" Robby Cummings

- "I am Loved" Mack Brock

- "The Blessing" Kari Jobe

- "God Really Loves Us" Dante Bowe

- "I AM" Eddie James

- "The Table" Jonathan Traylor

- "Defender" Jesus Culture

- "Psalm 23" Jason Upton

- "Cut to the Heart" Luke Partridge

- "You're Watching Over Me" Jason Upton

- "Father, Son, Spirit "Jason Upton

- "Whisper" Jason Upton

- "New Wine" Hillsong Worship

- "Rescue Song" Lauren Daigle

- "Champion" Bethel Music & Dante Bowe

- "No Limits" Harborside Music

- "Angels" Elle Limebear

- "Dancing on the Waves" Bethel Music

- "Write Every Day Down" Jason Upton

- "The Blessing" Kari Jobe

- "Psalm 139" Shane & Shane

- "Search Me" Sarah Reeves

- "Peace Be Still" Lauren Daigle

Pastor Eddie James

Revival Songs

- "We Want Revival Now" Catherine Mullins
- "Old Church Choir" Zach Williams
- "Let Your Glory Fall" Kari Jobe
- "Heartbeat" Beckah Shae
- "People Get Ready" Misty Edwards
- "The War Call" Luke Partridge
- "Strike the Ground" Elpis Spring
- "You're An Army" Rick Pino
- "Lord of the Harvest" Lindy Cofer
- "Let the Light In" Kari Jobe
- "All Creation" James Block
- "Revivals In the Air" Bethel Music & Melissa Helser
- "I Am a Voice" Rick Pino
- "Dancing on the Waves" Bethel Music
- "The Lion Tribe" Luke Partridge
- "People Get Ready" Misty Edwards
- "Mark My Hands" Lindy & The Circuit Riders
- "Start Right Here" Casting Crowns
- "Getting Ready" Maverick City Music & Upperroom

- "Thy Kingdom Come" Francesca Battistelli and Rita Springer

- "Walk in the Promise" Jeremy Riddle

- "Rise Up" Cain

- "Another Wave" Lindy Conant and the Circuit Riders

- "What Would You Do" Elevation Worship

Luke Partridge

SARA C GEORGE

Garden Songs

- "The Garden" Kari Jobe
- "Roses" Andrew Ripp
- "Tend" Emmy Rose Bethel Music
- "Back to the Garden" Crowder
- "Music from a Garden" The Gray Havens
- "Springtime" Chris Renzema
- "Garden of Love" Robby Cummings
- "Garden" Misty Edwards
- "Glory of Eden" David and Nicole Binion
- "Graves into Gardens" Elevation Worship
- "The Garden Song" John Denver
- "In the Garden" Alan Jackson
- "In the Garden" Anthem Lights
- "Love Note" UPPERROOM
- "Let This Garden Grow" Sarah Edwards, Audra Lynn & Chris Carr
- "Look What You've Done" Tasha Layton
- "Seasons" Benjamin William Hastings
- "Roses will Bloom Again" Juliet Serenio

- "Edens" Amanda Cook
- "The Beautiful Garden of Prayer" Into the Light
- "Green Garden Laura Mvula

Natalie George

Discussion Notes

Why We Train

Additional Reference:

YouTube <u>Here Comes Another Wave, Harvest Time</u>:
<u>https://www.youtube.com/watch?v=r64nemASz7M</u>

<u>Sara George's Love Notes from Heaven</u>

GOD's heart is for a mature bride to bring in a lost generation through Revival. He desires that not even one person will be lost and die an eternal death. Many people have not had an opportunity to hear the Gospel and know the truth of His love and salvation. Many churches do not teach about the Holy Spirit and His true nature. It is time for change. Generations have been lost due to moral decline including an increased number of parents who are lost, oppressed, and addicted. Christianity is different from other beliefs because of Jesus Christ. When many people say "God," they will acknowledge a god, but we cannot be sure they are acknowledging the one and only YAHWEH. In my personal opinion I suggest when you minister to and pray, with unbelievers include the name of Jesus as compelled, praying "in Jesus' Name", and thanking Jesus afterward.

Many people are crying out, seeking God, and asking Him for a rescue plan. The question is, "Will you allow God to use you to be a part of His solution?" If the answer is "Yes," that is why you should be willing to take your training seriously. In the harvest season, there will be assignments for all who seek the Lord and surrender to their blueprints. It is the Joshua 1:16-18 season. Matthew chapter 20 reveals that during the harvest, The Master will hire ALL who are waiting for work.

Participation in the Kingdom of God is imperative to hear His voice. There are many ways God can communicate with believers. God is always speaking, so let's go on a journey together to practice listening for God's voice.

I challenge you to pray and seek God to teach you new languages. Not everyone will hear in the same way, but find out how God is speaking to you. Search for His voice. We need to get to a place where we can stop the thoughts in our minds and analyze their origin. In the beginning stages of this process, it will start with emotions. Whenever you find yourself overwhelmed with emotion, you can trace it back to a series of thoughts. You then determine if the thoughts are negative or positive, scriptural or unscriptural. Sometimes, you hear a voice, and the words sound okay, but we need to recognize that if it brings confusion and questioning into your mind, the thought should still be tested. The bad guy always tries to disguise himself. If the outcome of the instruction or thought brings "bad fruit," it is not of God. If it brings the fruits of the Spirit, then you can start to see the difference.

Gifts are always the Holy Spirit working through you, and it is never you, although you are the conduit or vessel. Don't take God's glory or praise by saying, "I did this or that,", YOU did nothing, but witness the Holy Spirit do what only He can do. It is incorrect to tell someone who received a spiritual gift, "I'm so proud of you," because it has nothing to do with them. You are simply privileged to be a witness to God's power and Word. Gifts are distributed in God's timing, and for His specific assignments. He always equips the called.

They are tools for purpose and not for elevation. No single person is any more special than another. Try to remember we are all equipped with different gifts, and don't put God in a box by saying He can't do something. You can pray and seek gifts, and if God sees them as necessary to your calling in His time and season, they may be granted. Paul says anyone who speaks in tongues should pray for the gift of interpretation. If you speak in tongues, have you asked for the gift of interpretation?

The Voice of God can be found in many creative ways.

Here are some examples:

1. Visual imagery through images, such as words or pictures of yourself performing a task, dreams, and full visions.

2. Journaling, songwriting, or writing can bring words from God and clarity to situations.

3. Numbers and repetition.

4. Scripture highlighting and revelation.

5. Prayer/conversation/friendship/prophetic words.

6. Download/osmosis type of words spoken directly from the Holy Spirit/God.

7. Through creation itself – animals, signs, and wonders in nature. Ask God to show you a confirmation through nature.

8. Sounds and vibrations.

9. Movement such as dancing.

Section 2 Journal Notes

But the godly will flourish like palm trees and grow strong like the cedars of Lebanon. For they are transplanted to the Lord's own house. They flourish in the courts of our God. Even in old age they will still produce fruit; they will remain vital and green.

-Psalm 92:12-14 NLT

ABOUT THE AUTHOR

Sara George was born to live as a light, glowing, sparkling, and fragrant. She is a lovely, precious, shining, bold one planted in the beauty of Yahweh.

She is a daughter, wife, mother to many, gardener (her rose garden is spectacular and bountiful, the source of one of her ministries mentioned in the book), sister, friend, mentor, photographer (many of the photographs in this book are her own work), author, dancer, cook, artist, business owner, and a Jesus Partner expanding her tent pegs wherever he leads her to go and with whatever adventure he puts in her path. Although her identity is multifaceted, like a diamond, her life purpose is one – to expand the kingdom of heaven through truth, light, and love offering a pleasing aroma on the altar.

She is a Central Arkansas native and continues living in "The Ark" discipling the next generation as she worships King Jesus.

Sara Catherine George

1102 Ferguson Drive Benton, AR 72015

sara@lovenotesfromheaven.com

www.lovenotesfromheaven.com

YouTube Sara George's Love Notes From Heaven:

https://www.youtube.com/@sarageorgeslovenote

www.ingramcontent.com/pod-product-compliance
Lightning Source LLC
Chambersburg PA
CBHW051305120626
46547CB00015B/2093